My Kind of Midwest

My Kind of Midwest

Omaha to Ohio

JOHN A. JAKLE

The Center for American Places
at Columbia College Chicago

in association with
The Elizabeth Firestone Graham Foundation

Copyright © 2008 The Center for American Places at
Columbia College Chicago
All rights reserved
Published 2008. First edition.
Printed in China on acid-free paper.

The Center for American Places at Columbia College Chicago
600 South Michigan Avenue
Chicago, Illinois 60605-1996, U.S.A.
www.americanplaces.org

Distributed by the University of Chicago Press
www.press.uchicago.edu

16 15 14 13 12 11 10 09 08   1 2 3 4 5

Library of Congress Cataloging-in-Publication Data

Jakle, John A.
  My kind of Midwest : Omaha to Ohio / John A. Jakle. -- 1st ed.
       p. cm.
  Includes bibliographical references.
  ISBN 978-1-930066-87-8
  1. Middle West--Description and travel. 2. Middle West--Geography. 3. Middle West--
Social life and customs--Anecdotes. 4. Regionalism--Middle West. 5. Group identity--Mid-
dle West. 6. Jakle, John A.--Travel--Middle West. 7. Middle West--Biography. I. Title.

  F355.J35 2008
  917.704'33--dc22
                                   2008034126

  ISBN-10: 1-930066-87-2
  ISBN-13: 978-1-930066-87-8

Frontispiece: Downtown Chicago, as seen from Columbia College Chicago.
Photograph © 2008 by William Frederking and used by permission.

"In this region I am always stirred or appealed to by something which I cannot explain. The air seems lighter, the soil more grateful; a sense of something delicately and gracefully romantic is abroad."

—Theodore Drieser, *A Hoosier Holiday* (1916)

For Cindy

CONTENTS

In geographic extent, the American Midwest lends itself to ready defi-
nition. Most Americans agree that it comprises parts, if not all, of
twelve states: Ohio, Michigan, Indiana, Illinois, Wisconsin, Iowa, Minnesota, North and South Dakota, Nebraska, Kansas, and Missouri. This
is a diverse area, hardly homogeneous in any sense. In terms of physiog-
raphy, the Midwest includes not only the prairies of central Illinois and
plains of western Kansas, but also the Appalachian hills of southern
Ohio, the Ozark Mountains of Missouri, and the outliers of the Canadian
Shield in the Upper Great Lakes. In cultural terms, the Midwest has a
population of diverse origin. Its native inhabitants were first joined by
French, Spanish, and British colonists and then overwhelmed by Americans (with roots primarily in the British Isles, Central Europe, and Scan-
dinavia) as well as migrants coming directly from Europe. So also came
African-Americans and, more recently, Asians and Latinos. How could
the Midwest, as a region, possibly have a personality all its own?

Most Americans, nonetheless, consider that the Midwest does,
indeed, possess an identity, one that occupies a unique niche in the
national psyche different from that of New England, the South, or the
West, for example. The region's residents are thought of as somehow
typical of the nation as a whole. As the Midwest is the nation's "Heartland," it stands somehow as "quintessentially American."[1] It is certainly
not the region's environmental or cultural uniqueness that informs such

thinking, however. There are few attributes, physical or social, that only the Midwest possesses. Probably it is more a matter of how Midwesterners think and act in addition to what they would have others believe. As essayist Scott Russell Sanders suggested, the Midwest may be more a thing of inner landscapes than an outer world of physical and social actualities.[2] Likewise, as historian John E. Miller argued, the best way to understand the Midwest is to explore biographies of its people, and thus to probe the Midwest as an "imagined community." One needs to understand the "vocabulary," he wrote, that Midwesterners themselves use to explain "who they are and what their purposes are."[3]

The Midwest is an important place to me, and herein I share some of the reasons why. Place does not solely define what one becomes or dictate the values that one has, but place does provide the setting for one's socialization, helping to set the parameters within which one tends to act. "To argue that place matters and that peoples' origins have a significant influence on the types of person they become, is not to argue that all are affected in an identical fashion," John Miller wrote.[4] But I would emphasize that there is much that is commonly shared when a distinctive "sense of place" looms large in people's thinking. In the essay that follows, it is the various Midwestern "senses" of place that I treat. That is not to say that I do not consider real things that are observable in the Midwestern scene, but I emphasize more their symbolic value as they relate to mind-sets that I suspect are widely shared.

I was born in Indiana, raised in Michigan, and have lived and worked for decades in Illinois. I do not claim to be the typical Midwesterner but only a person well-rooted in the region. As a geographer, I proceed by juxtaposing my encounters with Midwestern landscapes and places with what I know of Midwestern history. Thus, I do seek to locate myself emotionally and intellectually within my native region. Regional identity, historians Andrew Cayton and Susan Gray have observed, is a form of storytelling.[5]

Contained herein are some of my stories about being a Midwesterner. A word of caution, therefore, seems appropriate. This book differs from the geographer's usual take on the world. It is the imagined Midwest (the region as it is "thought to be") that I emphasize. My mission is to get readers to think about geography not only as something objectively found "out there," but as something subjectively held in the mind as well. This book is about feelings, affectations, and values: personal impressions as they relate to the objective world of geographical study. Readers, I hope, will be challenged to locate themselves better within their own worlds of imagined landscapes and places.

My Kind of Midwest

It was a life-defining moment. Late in 1943, as a rather rambunctious four-year old, I began my career as a student of landscape. I remember the moment vividly, although I must admit that retelling the story to my students over the years led sometimes to a little embellishment. World War II was in full swing, but my mother and an aunt had accumulated sufficient gas ration coupons to drive from Terre Haute, Indiana, eastward fifteen miles to the city of Brazil to visit cousins. We drove along US 40, the old National Road, in what was my first car trip in open country. Excitedly, I bounced around. And then it happened. From the front, my mother, exhausted by the commotion, turned and said: "Be quiet! Look out the window!" But there was more. She began to point out things. Of course, there was the modern highway recently "four-laned," but there were also bits and pieces of relic road along the highway's margins. The highlight of all was the electric railway, a defunct "interurban" that ran to Indianapolis. At intervals, box motors stood motionless as if abruptly abandoned in place. I was fascinated. We were following a path with a clearly visible historical depth, or so I would come to conceptualize the experience much later. I was much too young then to understand things quite that way, but it did occur to me that mine was a changing world. "Things changed," I thought, "They did not always stay the same! What could it mean?"

We lived in Michigan—first in Grand Rapids, then in Detroit, and finally in a Detroit suburb. But between 1943 and 1946 my mother and I traveled several times each year to Terre Haute to spend time with my grandfather, Edward, and my aunt, Eugenie, who tended to him in his declining years. My mother and I would board a Pullman in Detroit's Michigan Central Station well before the train's departure, to awaken the next morning in Indianapolis. And then it was on to Terre Haute, looking out the window mostly from a dining car. After my grandfather died, the house from which my mother had gone off to college was sold. But frequently through the mid-1950s, my parents, with me in tow, went back by car to Terre Haute to visit friends, driving on to southern Illinois where relatives still lived. From Detroit we drove west to Coldwater along Michigan's old Chicago Pike. Then it was south to Fort Wayne and Indianapolis before turning west on US 40, back to the city that my father persistently called "Terry Hut." The next day we would drive on to Effingham, Illinois, and then turn south to Du Quoin, the town where my mother lived as a small child. Thus, at intervals, did I have the chance to observe changes along a traverse of the Midwest.

These trips by car were very important opportunities for the family's decompression. I was a child born to parents rather late in their lives. (My father was forty when I was born. In contrast, I was forty when my first grandchild arrived.) My parents were very much set in life's routines and very demanding of their only child. Home life was far from humorless, yet there was constant pressure to excel in ways that I was not fully equipped to handle at the time. But when we traveled, life seemed very different. Discipline was relaxed. Expectations changed, and life became truly enjoyable. The adults of my mother's family would sit reminiscing for hours when visiting one another. They relished remembering what life had once been like. Usually the only child present (my first cousins were fifteen to twenty years older), I would sit in the background quietly listening. The family's rise from poverty to degrees of real affluence sounded, as indeed it was, the very essence of success in America, and it had happened largely in the Midwest.

By age ten, I was convinced that the truly interesting times lay mainly in life's rearview mirror. Of course, it was not true. Nonetheless, the power of recollection was forcefully brought home to me. The past counted. It could not be denied. For me, it begged to be investigated. I would eventually decide that, if I could not know the past firsthand, at least I could know it vicariously by becoming something of a historian.

Certainly, one's intellectual inclinations reflect one's upbringing, and upbringing is always informed by either family history or a family's version of its history. Given my academic training, I was determined to avoid the pitfalls of family nostalgia: stories collected in antiquarian fashion suffused as much with myth as with fact. I avoided family genealogy for years. Then, by accident, I discovered an intriguing read in a used bookstore, Theodore Dreiser's *A Hoosier Holiday*.[1] The book details a 1915 motor trip that Dreiser and two companions made from New York City to Indiana: a "pilgrimage," Dreiser called it, whereby he could explore his roots by revisiting the places where he grew up as a boy. Becoming an author, he explained, might or might not have had something to do with those places. He did not know, but he owed it to himself to find out.

What occupied Dreiser on a three-week adventure to write a book had been occupying me for years. As a scholar, with publications of my own, I had come to comprehend the Midwest generally and Indiana specifically, much as Dreiser had. *A Hoosier Holiday* emphasized the highway (and the new mobility of motoring), the small town (and its community as something fundamental to the American experience), the city (emerging as a new, more important future), and the farm (as an anchor of American culture). I had come to the same landscape and place understandings in characterizing the Midwest as a distinctive section of the nation.[2]

"I can think of nothing more suited to my temperament then automobiling," Dreiser wrote. "It supplies just the mixture of change in fixity which satisfies me, leaves me mentally poised in inquiry, which always is delightful."[3] He was intrigued by the new infrastructure of auto travel. "It . . . dawned on me what an agency for the transmission of information and a certain kind of railway station gossip the modern garage has become," he quipped.[4] More than a half-century later, I found myself in full agreement. I had become intrigued, even as a boy, with what scholars now call the "roadside." On the repeated trips across Michigan, Indiana, and Illinois, I had taken to collecting petroleum company road maps (a different brand of gas at every stop) and had insisted on eating at every new drive-in (especially hamburgers and milk shakes). I relished staying at both downtown hotels and the new edge-of-city motels that were cropping up along America's highways like mushrooms during a moist spring. Should it really surprise that, much later, as a scholar, I would write books and articles on the impact of the nation's new automobility on its landscapes and places?[5]

Dreiser drove to Buffalo, New York, and Cleveland, Ohio, and then into Indiana by way of Fort Wayne. Then came the string of Indiana locations where he had lived: Warsaw, Terre Haute, Sullivan, Evansville, and Bloomington. Warsaw, where Dreiser began grade school, was his paragon for comprehending America's small towns, or at least its county-seat towns:

> Assemble four or five hundred frame and brick houses of slightly varying size and architecture and roominess, surround them with trees and pleasing grass plots, provide the town a main street and one cross street of stores, place one or two brick school houses at varying points in them, add one white sandstone courthouse in a public square, and a railroad sta-

tion, and four or five or six brick churches, and there you have them all. Give one town a lake, another a stream, another a mill pond—it makes little difference.[6]

Dreiser was very much interested in the relationship between small-town America and the nation's big cities. New York City had become his home. Much like Sherwood Anderson, Sinclair Lewis, and other prominent authors of the day, he had come to think of small-town life as very parochial.[7] "The small mind of the townsman is antipolar to that of the larger, more sophisticated wisdom of the city," he wrote. Perhaps the "still pools and backwaters of communal life as represented by these places," he continued, were necessary to the "preservation of the state of society." He did not know for sure, but he was certain that the "larger visioned" needed something to look down on, and small towns would do. Even as a boy, Warsaw had seemed confining, especially when he gazed at, "The people who went to Chicago, or Evansville, or Terra Haute, or Indianapolis!" sitting in the windows of passing passenger trains. A place such as Brazil, Indiana, "a mere shabby coal town of town of three or four thousand population," seemed something wonderful, he remembered.[8] Often he had fantasized about being on a train. Where might he be going? What would he do when he got there?

Irony of ironies, Dreiser found that cities, for their presumed superiority, were also easily stereotyped and were frequently very much like small towns.[9] With the exception of New York City and Chicago, few American cities seemed to him to be truly distinctive. Fort Wayne he thought only "a humble copy of every other American city in all that it attempted: streets, cabarets, high buildings and so on."[10] There was little of interest. On reaching Terre Haute, however, where his father had once operated a grain mill, things struck him as more upbeat. It was exciting to be there. Perhaps it was pride in his family's connection. Terre Haute was a factory city. Smoke filled the air, there being "a somewhat inspiriting display of chimneys and manufacturing buildings in one direction and another" (See Fig. 1 on pages 70–71 in *Gallery: The Midwest in Pictures*). The sound of engine bells and factory whistles in the evening at six o'clock indicated to him "a cheerful prosperity."[11] Before arriving at Evansville, he had "brushed up" on his local geography, mentally creating a list of things he wanted to see: not only the various houses where his family had lived, but also the church and school he attended and the Ohio River at the foot of Main Street, where, on one January day playing with friends, he had fallen through the ice and nearly perished.[12]

He found the Midwestern countryside, when compared with that in the East, relatively monotonous. Seemingly everywhere were "houses with low fences and prominent chicken coops, orchards laden with apples of a still greenish yellow color, fields of yellowing wheat or corn, but 'oh so flat.'" But the region's rural landscapes were also "profoundly endearing."[13] Dreiser's party stopped along a highway in Ohio just to relax. In a green pasture, they tossed a ball around. "It was so hot and still that even insects seemed to have taken cover," he wrote. Looking up, Dreiser saw a buzzard soaring on an afternoon thermal. "Truly this is my own, my native land," he said. "I have rejoiced in hundreds of days just like this," he enthused. It was so very much Midwestern: "the sleepy, baking atmosphere of summer heat, high humidity, and hazy sky."[14] In northern Indiana, he found a land of smooth, undulating terrain and fertile soils, small but comfortable houses, large barns painted gray or red, the American silo, the American style of windmill, and the American motor car: "a happy land of public schools, Sunday schools, and churches." As part of the Midwest, northern Indiana was a place anchored "in a faith in God and humanity as laid down by the Presbyterian or the Baptist or the Methodist Church and by the Ten Commandments"—all of which, Dreiser admitted, was "at once reassuring and yet disturbing."[15]

Did Dreiser's trip achieve its purpose? He never says. But those familiar with *Sister Carrie* or *An American Tragedy*, among his other novels, can readily recognize the childhood roots of much of this writing.[16] The Dreiser family, as the name suggests, was of German origin. Theodore's father was something of an entrepreneur, but alcoholism undermined his business endeavors. The family moved frequently in response to what seemed a never-ending string of bad luck. His older brother, Paul, ran away from home as a teenager, changed his name to Dresser, and became one of the nation's most celebrated songwriters. "On the Banks of the Wabash" and "My Gal Sal" were inspired by Dresser's days in Terre Haute and Evansville (and nights spent, pundits like to emphasize, in the red-light districts of both cities). Theodore, after an uneventful year at Indiana University, came of age as a newspaper reporter, first in St. Louis, Missouri, then in Toledo and Cleveland, Ohio, and finally in New York City.

For me, *A Hoosier Holiday* became a mirror into which I could gaze in order to understand better my own roots. Dreiser's task was to know himself, to validate who he was as a popular commentator on the American scene. My approach to the Midwest, on the other hand, had been much less impelling. Indeed, until I read *A Hoosier Holiday*, it had been fully unfocused. My preoccupation had been simply to know the past. "What would it have been like to have been there?" I asked. As a scholar, I wanted to travel to the geographical past, perhaps something akin to what H. G. Wells called "time travel."[17] Thus, I set about exploring other people's past experiencing of landscape and place, investigating what they had cared to write down, map, draw, or make photographs of what they had seen. I think it a truism that we form our geography, and that afterward our geography forms us. Certainly, we imagine our geography, and that helps guide what we become. What was it, I wanted to know, that past geography had collectively predisposed in America? What were the lessons to be learned?

What my mother's people talked about in family gatherings galvanized my interest in things historical, taking on almost epic implications. Victor and Irma Allais, with their two daughters and four sons, landed in New York City in the early 1880s, led by their oldest son, Florent, then in his mid-twenties. For generations, the male members of the family had been coal miners, the family moving from town to town along the coal vein that straddled the Belgian-French border near Lille before the journey from Marles-les-Mines, the small French mining town where my grandfather, Edward, was born, to Antwerp by train, then by boat to Hull, and train again to Liverpool, where passage to America was arranged. Told of work in western Pennsylvania, they detrained at Noblestown, near Pittsburgh, their savings nearly exhausted. There on a cold winter night, in a small rental cottage without furniture, they spread their bedrolls out on the hard floor. The miner's wages offered them were no better than they had known in France, and living conditions were far worse. Through tears of anguish they determined to return to Europe at the first opportunity. Such was not to be. After several months, they moved on to Indiana. At Brazil, where a small French-speaking community had assembled, Edward Allais went to work in the mines at age sixteen.

Edward's younger brother, Arthur, took an interest in religion, and members of the local Methodist Church took an interest in him. They arranged for English lessons, seeing in Arthur a means of accessing the town's staunchly Roman Catholic French community. While Edward dug coal and helped support his brother, Arthur attended Depauw University. He graduated and was ordained a Methodist minister, going off to Chicago and a missionary church in a French-speaking neighborhood on the West Side. The charismatic young minister soon found a buyer for coal that Edward and other relatives were then mining on their own, the family having learned the art of sinking mine shafts.

Then came opportunity for the family to create new mines for a Chicago investor syndicate, first in western Indiana at Mecca, north of Terre Haute, and then in southern Illinois at what became the town of Christopher, east of Du Quoin. The United Coal Company—in which Arthur, Edward, and cousin Frank Urbain held an equity interest—laid out the town of Christopher, stocked its first store, and sank two mine shafts some six miles apart, connecting them underground in what became one of the nation's largest coal mines (Fig. 2).

Just prior to World War I, the Allais brothers created a coal company of their own. Its very name, the Columbus Mining Company, spoke forcefully of New World beginnings. The firm purchased several mines at Brazil, including the mines where Edward had first worked as a teenager, and then it opened several new mines closer to Terre Haute. It was in Terre Haute where my grandparents chose to reside (Fig. 3), though the bulk of the firm's operations ultimately came to center at Hazard in the eastern mountains of Kentucky.

Growing up I knew almost nothing about my father's family, the surviving members of which had gravitated to the West Coast. We seldom visited them. It was not until the 1980s, when Jakle cousins interested in genealogy discovered me, that I finally learned about my father's people. Felix Jakle (from Baden, Germany) and his wife, Mary (from Basel, Switzerland), came to the United States following the aborted 1848 Revolution. He was a shoemaker displaced by the rise of factory-made shoes in Germany. Unfortunately, the days of the self-employed cobbler

14

were nearly over in the United States as well. Landing in New York City, they settled briefly in Cleveland, Ohio. The family moved on to Terre Haute, and then to Effingham, where a sizable German-speaking community had assembled. With relatives, Felix worked to establish one of the nation's earliest lager breweries. Brewing was then only a winter occupation (lager beer requiring cooling), and during the summer months, so census documents say, he worked as a landscape gardener. Prior to learning this, I had not even known my great-grandparents' names. The Jakles did not look back to tell fond stories. Tuberculosis had struck the family, taking Mary first, then Felix, and eventually five of their ten children (Fig. 4). Of the surviving siblings, only Martin chose to live in Effingham, opening a bakery across from the Effingham County courthouse. Brothers August, Louis, and Edward ended up in St. Louis, and John, my grandfather, returned to Terre Haute.

John, and his doings in Terre Haute, are why Theodore Dreiser's *A Hoosier Holiday* resonates so strongly with me. From the late-1880s through Prohibition, this John Jakle ran a saloon on Terre Haute's Ohio Street, near the Vigo County courthouse. Being a saloon keeper was a step down from being a brewmaster. Nonetheless, it was a worthy occupation, especially in Terre Haute with its large beer-drinking German community. I know now that lowly paid typographers, a highly migratory class of newspapermen, called the saloon "Jakle Chapel."[1] Union organizing took place there, and it was a meeting place for Terre Haute's socialists. My father's father was very much a socialist by political persuasion and, thus, very much a labor sympathizer (Fig. 5).

My father, also named John, rejected his father's socialist politics. He became a staunch Republican and came to admire greatly his extroverted father-in-law, the capitalist coal operator, Edward Allais. As a curious teenager recently arrived in the United States, my mother's father, having attended several political rallies, was asked: "Are you going to be a Republican or a Democrat?" "A Republican," he is said to have retorted. "I like the way they dress."

My father pursued a career in corporate sales. During World War II, his company held patent rights to an aluminum treatment process necessary in aircraft manufacture. When Detroit's auto plants converted to war production, we moved to the "Motor City." On occasion, I accompanied him to various defense plants: Budd Wheel, Cadillac Main, Fisher Body, Dodge Main, and, most impressive of all, Ford's gigantic Willow Run. It was the largest factory ever built specifically to meet a nation's war needs. Aircraft were mass-produced on an assembly line in much the same manner as motor cars.

My father's mother, Minnie Bischoff, was also of German descent. Her father, Jacob Bischoff, was a wagon maker in St. Louis, and two of his sons are reputed to have been the last teamsters in St. Louis to operate horse-drawn wagons. As a child, my dad spent his summers in St. Louis, most days accompanying one of his teamster uncles on delivery rounds. What he remembered most vividly was the bustling waterfront with its brick warehouses and factory lofts set apart from the Mississippi River by the cobbled levee along which steamboats moored. The scene is very different today (Fig. 6).

Theodore Dreiser and his companions visited his old school, St. Joseph's on Ohio Street, when in Terre Haute. They might have lifted a beer at John Jakle's saloon, since it was located across and just down the street from the school playground. On the banks of the Wabash River, four blocks away, my grandfather kept a houseboat. There the typographers, newly arrived in town, stayed until more permanent quarters could be arranged. The newspaper connection proved important for my father. Beginning as an eight-year-old, he had a paper route for the *Terre Haute Tribune.* Dreiser, a former newspaperman, might have stopped at the newspaper office on one of those August evenings of 1915. If he had, he may have seen my father, a sixteen-year-old, handling the night telephone on the home delivery desk.

Today, the site where the saloon once stood sports a drive-in bank, the original building torn down in the 1960s for a parking lot.

The school is still there. The mill that Theodore Dreiser's father once operated (close to where my grandfather's houseboat was moored) was demolished nearly a century ago, when Terre Haute's riverfront was wiped clean during the first of several rounds of urban renewal. Return to the neighborhoods where the Dreisers once lived (Ninth and Chestnut or Twelfth and Walnut) and you do not find the humble working-class houses that once stood there. Only commercial buildings and vacant lots greet the eye now. One house associated with the Dreisers still stands but not at its original location. In the 1920s, the house where brother Paul was born was moved to a city park. There it sits as a memorial to him, looking very much out of place. Only in recent decades was Theodore remembered publicly but only with a historical marker. The Dreiser family produced a literary giant, a son who made it his business to document and interpret life in his family's adopted country.

Few people write down their thoughts about life or have their thoughts written down by others. Save through the cryptic entries of census ledgers, directory listings, public land records, newspaper obituaries, and the like do most Americans enter the written historical record at all. At best, what people leave behind are the physical or material traces of where they once lived, worked, or played. For most people, the material culture of a landscape represents their only archive, and many people do not leave even that. Late-in-life awareness of my father's family took me to Terre Haute and to the small library of the local historical society, located in what was once an elegant townhouse. I found city directory entries but, beyond that, little directly relevant to the Jakle past: only a few photographs of Ohio Street showing at a distance my grandfather's saloon. Looking up from my work, however, I glanced out a window across various backyards. There, on the left, was the back door of the Allais house. On the right, and slightly down a side street, was the front door of the Jakle house. No wonder my parents came to know one another. Such opportune propinquity!

Youthful treks across the Midwest with my parents piqued my interest in many aspects of geography. For example, there were the small towns. Highway driving, as Dreiser asserted, could get monotonous when all one saw were open fields and farmsteads at a distance. But at regular intervals our motoring was punctuated by "Main Streets," the very town centers that Sinclair Lewis painted as dull, but which I found to be full of excitement. One entered and left town usually along a tree-lined street bordered by comfortable houses: two-story frame dwellings more to the north in the Midwest and single-story or story-and-a-half bungalows more to the south. Farther out were new commercial strips just aborning. There, businesses mainly served motorists (gas stations, tourist courts, and drive-in restaurants, for example), although there were the occasional implement yards and new farm service stores as well. I was appointed the map reader and navigator on family trips, even though my father knew the roads very well and could have driven them in his sleep. He had been over them innumerable times as a salesman.

Dropping out of college when Prohibition closed the family business and brought on hard times, my father first sold slide advertising (to be projected on screens of small-town movie theaters) along routes deep into the American South. Then he went to work for Ralston Purina selling seed and feed across Indiana and Illinois. He sold coal mining equipment across central Illinois and then, after my parents married, coal for Columbus Mining across southern Michigan, before taking up chemical sales during World War II. As we traveled southward from Detroit in the late-1940s and early-1950s, he would muse: "I wonder if Jim Davis [or whomever] is still around." Then we would go into a grain elevator, chicken hatchery, or coal yard, and there my father would be greeted, always with much affection, even if it had been ten or fifteen years since he had last "dropped by." I witnessed the same collegiality when we overnighted at Terre Haute in the big downtown hotel, the Terre Haute House. Within half a block of leaving the hotel, someone would recognize him and call him by name, even though he had not resided in the city for decades.

My mother's family was involved in actually creating small towns. Not just Christopher in southern Illinois but nearby Coella, Buckner, and Urbain as well. My uncle Ed initially managed the company store at Christopher. As a student in mine engineering at Ohio State University, he had been called home to work when my grandfather learned that he was contemplating a contract to play pro ball for the St. Louis Cardinals' farm team in Columbus. He was a pitcher and a very good one. But, as a teenager, he had always played under an assumed name. My grandmother, a dedicated Calvinist, frowned on the frivolities of sport, especially on the Sabbath, when small-town teams played baseball in the early twentieth century.[1] At Christopher, my uncle married the railroad station agent's daughter, who worked for her father as a telegrapher. My aunt carried a pistol to and from work. Christopher was a male-dominated place and often quite violent, saloons quickly outnumbering stores on the town's main street. Numerous were the stories my relatives told of killing and mayhem in early Christopher. Mining towns in the Midwest were very much like those of the "Wild West." Indeed, many stereotypes from "western" history, are, in fact, rooted in the Midwest—in the male-dominated "cow towns" of Kansas, for example.

The Allais family lived in nearby Du Quoin, an older, larger, and more civil town located on the Illinois Central Railroad's main line. It was there that my family's annual auto trips terminated. The local newspaper, the *Du Quoin Call*, invariably carried a short announcement to the effect that several local families (including the Irish Kellys and the German Weinbergs, related to us through marriage) had visitors from Detroit. And there would be rounds of visits with friends my mother knew from grade school. Frequently, I would be stopped on the street and asked if I were not Irene's son. That never happened at home in Detroit. Was the Midwest small town some kind of extended family? Did everybody really know everybody else? And everyone else's business? My relatives owned a drugstore on Main Street, a great place to observe the town's comings and goings bent over the comic book rack.

I also learned to keep my eyes and ears open back home. I relished visits to my father's office on the twenty-fifth floor of the Penobscot Building. Late in his career, he switched to selling insurance, overseeing group insurance programs at Michigan Bell and other corporations. Thus, my first employment (during summers while in high school) was at the telephone company's downtown headquarters in its print shop. As a delivery boy, I quickly came to appreciate the differences between life on the executive level eighteen floors up and life in the mail room down in the basement. Michigan Bell's location adjacent to the city's blighted skid row provided another contrast. Once every morning and once every afternoon I took orders and ventured out, wending my way between aggressive streetwalkers and passed-out derelicts to the most extraordinary of greasy spoons, there to collect coffee and donuts. It was at this time that I obtained my first single-lens reflex camera and began to take seriously the shooting of photographs (Fig. 7).

What stands out in my mind about downtown Detroit, however, involves one particular trip, when I was quite young. From that single episode I carry a host of vivid images that together sum up for me just how exciting big cities in the nation's heartland once were, even cities such as today's Detroit, so badly blighted by "Rust Belt" woes. It was the last day of the baseball season, probably in 1948. We had the car radio on, listening to the Tigers play. The announcer, Harry Heilman (whose radio voice, it was said, could be heard on summer afternoons wherever traffic stopped for red lights between Toledo and the Straits of Mackinac), thanked his listeners for their loyalty. The Tigers had done poorly that year, but there would always be next year. Our car windows were down, as it was very hot that September day. Streetcars congested traffic, and the squeal of their wheels on the rails, the snap of overhead sparks on the wires, and the incessant grind of electric motors was constant. Flatbed trailer trucks carrying engine blocks, fenders, or even whole car bodies competed for position. We entered the first of several industrial zones that ringed the city center—passing Continental Motors, still a manufacturer of aircraft engines, and then the Hudson Motor Car Company, its buildings lining both sides of the street (Fig. 8). The windows of the engine plant were open on the immediate right, and, inside, men stood sweating at lathes turning and cutting metal. The noise was deafening.

Between industrial zones—each oriented to a railroad—were residential districts. The houses of each neighborhood became progressively older as we approached downtown. The towers of large churches stretched into the heavens, with names indicative of German, Irish, or Polish roots. Evident also was Italian and Greek ethnicity, especially on signs posted above the doors of grocery, confectionary, and other stores. But, close to downtown, people on the streets were mainly African-American. Here was "Paradise Valley," the black business district with its many dance halls, night clubs, gambling dens, and brothels, as well as its more "legitimate" commerce (Fig. 9). What I saw was something of the rural, small-town South but city-contained, a distinctly urban neighborhood. Memories of Detroit's 1943 race riot were still fresh ("Lock your door," my mother said as we passed through), and

22

visible were many vacant lots where buildings stood before arsonists had done their work. Detroit had mushroomed when, after World War I, the automobile industry boomed. So also did World War II bring prosperity, a welcomed circumstance following the economic doldrums of the Great Depression. As the nation's leading producer of trucks, jeeps, tanks, and aircraft engines, the city had dubbed itself "The Arsenal of Democracy." But all was not positive. Social tensions spawned in the American South and across eastern and southern Europe were brought to the city and then pushed to the breaking point. Blacks lived in segregated housing, restricted from moving much beyond the city's extremely overcrowded near East Side by deed covenants, realtor steering, bank redlining, and outright threats of violence.

Finally, we reached our downtown destination, the giant J. L. Hudson Department Store. Unable to find a parking place, my father and I waited in the car while my mother went inside. I was pleased. I disliked shopping (and still do). It could take my mother six or seven stores (and two or three hours) just to buy a new hat. Hudson's occupied an entire city block—only Macy's in Manhattan was larger. Hudson's was a Detroit institution and, as such, exercised much power. I learned many years later that it successfully blocked Sears and other retail chains from building downtown. And, decades later, it would be the mammoth suburban malls owned by Hudson's (Northland and Eastland, for example) that would eventually signal the end of retailing in the city's central business district.

In 1948, Hudson's olive green delivery trucks could be seen throughout the Detroit area, especially in more affluent suburbs, such as Grosse Pointe where my family lived. With World War II over, business was brisk, and deliveries were many, but new trucks were in short supply. So Hudson's continued in service its fleet of electric trucks built in the 1920s. Fascinated, I watched these chain-drive vehicles with open cabs quietly coming and going at the store's loading docks. Pedestrians swirled all around. Newspaper boys shouted out the headlines, "Tigers

Lose in Season Finale." A mounted policeman passed slowly by. In the distance, rag men in horse-drawn wagons (truly the last "teamsters") moved in and out of alleys. It was as if I had been transported back several decades without using a time machine. But everywhere there were cars. Those parked around were stacked two deep at the curb. Auto horns blared incessantly. Auto exhaust permeated the air.

Detroit was an exciting city, but Chicago was an exciting metropolis (Fig. 10). Chicago was not only much bigger, but was held together by a mature mass transit system as well as by auto use. Downtown excitement was amplified a hundred times, or so I thought, by the rattle, screech, and hum of the "El" (sometimes called the "L"), the elevated electric line that looped around the city's downtown core. Encouraged out along the elevated tracks and along the commuter railroads, as well, was apartment living in buildings large and small (Fig. 11). Chicago's neighborhoods were densely built with double- and triple-decked flats, duplexes, and bungalows tightly packed together.

Driving into Chicago from the east, we passed through the industrial suburbs of northwestern Indiana, each with its dominant industry (steel at Gary and oil refining at Whiting, for example). Surface streets were poorly coordinated between municipalities, with the numbered highways (US 6, 12, or 20) handling out-of-town traffic more through afterthought than forethought. Crossing the Calumet River into Chicago, almost immediately there was an El station closely surrounded by retail buildings and, of course, apartment blocks. The city did not appear slowly as by stages, but it immediately hit me in the face as something fully splendid. We drove north along Lake Shore Drive, the impressive skyline of downtown looming up ahead. It was in Chicago that Columbus Mining was headquartered, high up in the McCormick Building on Michigan Avenue across from Grant Park (Fig. 12).

After World War II, downtown retailing began to shift north across the Chicago River and up Michigan Avenue. Dubbed the "Magnificent Mile," it is today lined with massive shopping complexes and hotel towers, the streets on either side lined with tall apartment and condominium buildings (Fig. 13). Spread farther north along the lake is the so-called "Gold Coast," Chicago's equivalent to New York City's Upper Eastside.

Chicago was the nation's premier railroad center, as it remains today. Passenger trains approaching the city crept slowly from one railroad yard to another, periodically rumbling over the "diamond" of one or another cross line, rows of boxcars obscuring the view more often than not. Once inside the city, however, trains ran on high embankments punctuated at intervals by concrete viaducts through which ran the major streets of the ubiquitous street grid. The railroads physically divided the city into somewhat isolated neighborhoods, with life in each area substantially focused inward.

The neighborhoods, while insular, were not static. By the 1950s, Poles had succeeded Germans and Swedes on the city's near North Side. Irish, Italians, Greeks, and Russian Jews competed for dominance on the near West Side. Black Chicago, very much like New York City's Harlem and Detroit's Paradise Valley, was tightly contained on the South Side. Land use in the Chicago area changed greatly in the decades after World War II. When my father sold chemicals, business took him frequently to South Wabash Avenue, specifically to an industrial loft building adjacent to the elevated tracks where the firm's chemicals were manufactured. Then the company moved out to a western suburb near the newly developed O'Hare Airport. Built there was a sprawling, single-story building with abundant room for future expansion. Friends of my parents lived just south of Chicago. Visits with them enabled me to watch the construction of the planned suburb of Park Forest, a place very similar to the several Levittowns outside of New York City and Philadelphia, also intended for returning war veterans and their families. Everything at Park Forest was oriented to the automobile: the new shopping center, the schools, the churches, and, of course, the miles and miles of houses that made the curvilinear streets with their cul-de-sacs look so very much alike. Other friends lived just north of Chicago in

Evanston, one of the city's older railroad suburbs. How the two suburbs differed: Park Forest was new, spread out, sun-parched, and, to my eyes, dreadfully dull; Evanston was old, compactly configured, tree-shaded, possessing real character as a place rooted in time. A watered-down Park Forest model dominated the building of most post-war Chicago suburbs (Fig. 14). It was that watered-down model that brought the seemingly endless sprawl, first to areas between the radii of the commuter railroads that fanned out from city center, and then to pre-viously undeveloped areas totally beyond the railroad's reach.[2]

My wife, Cynthia, and I married in 1957. We met in Grosse Pointe shortly before her father, a regional office manager for the Goodyear Tire and Rubber Company, transferred to Chicago. In our early married years, we frequently visited my in-laws on the city's far South Side. After Goodyear also moved to the O'Hare area, we visited them first in Elmhurst (a railroad suburb initially) and then at Elk Grove Village and Hoffman Estates (both fully auto-oriented). From the latter location, through the 1960s, I watched nearby Schaumburg grow from a German-American farm community into one of Chicago's "edge cities"—with office towers, shopping malls, numerous big-box stores, commercial strip development, hotels, huge apartment and condominium com-plexes, and, of course, sprawling housing estates (Fig. 15). Schaum-burg developers are just now getting around to providing a traditional downtown—still another shopping center but one configured to look like a small city's central business district fully rooted in the past.[3]

Cynthia's maiden name is Powell. That family's lineage in America stretches back to the founding of Jamestown in Virginia. Her father, Robert, was born and raised outside of Roanoke, Virginia, an old rail-road town. His father worked as an engineer on the Norfolk and West-ern Railroad and was also a part-time farmer. Cindy's mother, Catherine, was born in Troy, New York. Her family, the Maguires, emi-grated in the 1890s from Ireland's County Sligo. Thomas Maguire was also an engineer (but of stationary steam engines). He became a boiler tender at Troy's Burden Iron Works. Like the Powells, the Maguires were eventually attracted to the Midwest—specifically to Akron, a boom town very much tied to Detroit and the automobile industry. By World War I, Akron had become the rubber capital of the nation. Many of Cindy's relatives worked for one tire company or another. Akron became another place where, as a geographer, I could take the "pulse of the world." Or, less pretentiously, it was another vantage point for getting to know the Midwest.

Cindy's growing up was spread well over the map: Galesburg in Illinois, Bay City in Michigan, Cincinnati and Akron in Ohio, Birmingham in Alabama, Richmond in Virginia, and, eventually, Grosse Pointe. She was, admittedly, a "corporation brat." After we married, her odyssey continued: Ann Arbor and Kalamazoo in Michigan, Carbondale in Illinois, Bloomington in Indiana, Orono in Maine, back to Kalamazoo for a year, back to Carbondale for a summer, and, finally, to Urbana, Illinois, where we have managed to stay put for more than three decades.

Constant moving from place to place is quite common in America. Moving over great distances substantially undermines loyalty to, or identification with, any one section of the nation. In this regard, the Midwest may have suffered the most. Through the early twentieth century, Midwesterners—especially the college-educated—departed for places as diverse and as widely separated as New York City and Los Angeles. It was to Manhattan, after all, that Theodore Dreiser, like many writers, was drawn in search of fame. Both economically and culturally, the Midwest was largely "colonial" to New York City where control of the nation's financial capital centered. Important for Dreiser, the nation's publishing industry was centered there also. Like Detroit, Los Angeles was an early twentieth-century boom town and one equally as colonial, being energized through the making of such things as airplanes and motion pictures. But Hollywood made southern California a generator of popular culture, influencing everything from domestic architecture to dress, to auto styling. Los Angeles enjoyed mild climate, an attraction to those seeking health and recreation. Southern California was promoted as an Eden, giving impulse to Jakle cousins who, in the 1930s, packed up an old Graham-Page sedan and motored out to Los Angeles on Route 66.

Cindy and I have two daughters. Stephanie is a librarian at Pennsylvania State University and her husband, Hossein, is a mathematician there. Barbara, a professional photographer, lives in Omaha. Some people feel that western (and even central) Pennsylvania is very much like the Midwest. (Is not Penn State now a member of the Big Ten Conference?) Nebraska, of course, is very much Midwestern, at least until you reach the Sand Hills where the West seems to begin. Getting to and from Omaha by car takes us with regularity across Iowa, perhaps the most Midwestern of all states—at least for those who conceptualize the region mainly in rural terms. Many Iowans live and work on farms or in small towns. Even urban employment has a decidedly agrarian orientation: farm implement manufacturing, meat packing, and grain milling, for example. Motoring back and forth to Pennsylvania takes us through Ohio and through or around one or another of the state's many cities. Ohio may be the least Midwestern state, even for those who recognize the Midwest as urban as well as rural. Many of Ohio's small towns tend to look very "eastern." Around Cleveland in the "Western Reserve" (settled initially by Connecticut Yankees), one can find village greens, white Greek Revival cottages with green shutters, and tall-steepled churches, looking very much as if they belong in New England. Many older residential neighborhoods in Ohio's largest cities, with their now-dated workers' cottages and row houses, look like they belong more in Philadelphia or Baltimore. This is especially true of Cincinnati. Nonetheless, relatively little that is historic, or even historical, survives in Ohio's big-city downtowns. In Cincinnati, landmark buildings stand isolated in parking-lot surrounds (Fig. 16). The automobile, and its demand for space, clearly rules.

Geographer James Shortridge traced the history of the Midwest as a concept: the idea that there is some part of the United States called the "Midwest" (or Middle West) that stands distinctive from other sections of the nation.[4] According to Shortridge, the term was first coined in the 1880s to describe Kansas and Nebraska in the array of states and territories that ranged north-south through the Great Plains. But as the railroads extended westward, largely from Chicago, the idea came to be applied across a vast hinterland of natural resources and industrial production centered on Chicago. And that included, if I may expand upon his thinking somewhat, the area east of Chicago along the railroads as far as Ohio, if not well into western Pennsylvania.

Earlier geographical referents, such as the Ohio Valley and the Mississippi Valley, which were coined when river navigation provided the base for mid-continental commercial networking, declined in use with the coming of the railroads. Additionally, the Civil War and the events leading up to it firmly defined in American minds fundamental differences between North and South. The Ohio River, which once tied a vast territory together, came to serve in people's mental maps as a sectional dividing line instead. With railroading, of course, rivers became barriers to movement. River towns continued to thrive largely to the extent that they served, with their huge bridges of iron and steel, as river-crossing places.

The largest cities grew as industrial centers. And, as importantly, they became important distribution centers also, clusters of warehouses being interspersed amid the factories that lined waterfronts. So it was that Cincinnati, Louisville, and Evansville on the Ohio; St. Louis, St. Paul, and Minneapolis on the Mississippi; and Kansas City and Omaha on the Missouri came to function as gateway cities. These centers funneled the output of farms and mines located to the south or to the west into the nation's manufacturing belt with its highly specialized industrial urban centers, such as Detroit and Akron. As gateways, they also functioned as distribution points for manufactured goods moving the other way.

With much chagrin, I photographed the demolition of Omaha's "Jobber's Canyon," an artifact of that city's gateway role (Fig. 17). The wholesale houses that once supplied retailers across Nebraska and even Wyoming were concentrated just east of the railroad bridge over the Missouri River. Even though old buildings were destroyed, old economic implications remain, specifically the new corporate campus of one of the nation's largest food processors, Conagra. Just outside of Omaha is Offutt Air Force Base, built on the grounds of Fort Crook, an 1880s Army post. Headquartered at Offutt is the U.S. Strategic Command, which oversees the nation's defensive shield in what is now very much a nuclear age. Omaha was once on the nation's frontier and then on the edge of the manufacturing belt. It is now fully central not only in a geographical sense, but in a strategic military sense as well. Barbara's husband, Jim, a retired career officer in the Air Force, works at Offutt as a military planner. Omaha is also the American telemarketing capital, a role prompted, in part, by the Midwestern dialect spoken in the city. Omaha English resonates well across the nation. It is readily understood by all Americans. "Midland" speech patterns of the Midwest—an outgrowth of Pennsylvania speech of the colonial era—stands as another example of the Midwest's "middleness."

But the Midwest truly centers on Chicago, which stands above all the other cities at mid-continent as an industrial and distribution center and, more importantly, as a financial center. Historian William Cronon chronicled how Chicago interests, financed largely from New York City and Boston, captured the mid-continent's grain, cattle, and lumber markets—first through canal building and then through railroad construction.[5] Chicagoans perfected trade in commodity futures, thus revolutionizing not only the marketing of grain, but also the financing of grain production. Assembly-line procedures (dis-assembly lines, if you prefer) were perfected in the city's slaughterhouses and packing plants long before Henry Ford and his minions adapted assembly-line methods to car production at Detroit. As a twentieth-century industrial center, metropolitan Chicago was second only to Pittsburgh in iron and steel production; U.S. Steel's Illinois Works (in South Chicago) and its Indiana Works (at nearby Gary) were among the nation's largest. Chicago came to exceed all cities in meat packing (Swift and Armour are still well-remembered names), the manufacture of railroad equipment (Pullman), the making of farm implements (McCormick and Deering), and the printing of books and magazines (Donnelly). Nor was the city a slouch when it came to retailing: Montgomery Ward and Sears and Roebuck revolutionized mail-order selling with their catalogues, and Marshall Fields practically invented the department store. In areas other than business, Chicago gained renown as well. The city has long been the Midwest's principal cultural center, home to the Art Institute of Chicago and the Chicago Symphony Orchestra, for example. This cultural cache in combination with its nightlife has made it the Midwest's premier tourist and convention destination. Even Chicago's Union Stock Yards and its packing plants were once open to visitors.

Some scholars argue that what one learns in traveling from place to place can never match what native residents know. One has to live—and presumably work—in a place to know it well. Only then is knowledge of a place truly authentic. Travel, particularly of the touristic kind, has implicit in it a kind of superficial taking. Additionally, tourism can even be exploitative to the degree that tourists turn people and their places into curiosities to be consumed. Local people can be negatively impacted if only to the extent that they participate unwittingly in games of pretend calculated to pleasing visitors. Factory tours make industrial work floors into visual spectacles and, accordingly, workers into objects of curiosity.[1] When previously private spaces are made public or when the sacred is made profane, then the distinctive life of a locality can be easily trivialized and even destroyed. People who travel strictly as tourists often demean themselves, as well, through a spectator's delusion—by mistaking the tourist "gaze," as sociologist John Urry called it, for real participation.[2] Tourists easily mistake superficial seeing for understanding. Nonetheless, much of what people think they know about the world does come through firsthand validation obtained in travel, irrespective of how superficial observation might be. I have traveled the Midwest strictly as a tourist, seeking out with some regularity resort spots, such as the Lake Michigan shore. As a historical geographer, I have combined pleasure with work in such places as Galena,

Illinois, and Madison, Indiana—Midwestern towns with much historic architecture surviving from the mid-nineteenth century.

In our highly mobile world of expanded leisure time and relative affluence, Americans play the tourist role more often and for longer periods of time than most of us—especially those who abide a strong work ethic—are wont to admit. Recreational change of pace away from home and work has become very much a part of contemporary life. Across the United States, even in the Midwest, tourism ranks as a leading industry. Michigan, for example, is certainly an industrial state. Car-related manufacturing remains the state's leading employer, but for more than a century tourism has ranked as number two. Tourism is an important activity to study. I study it, but I am not immune from it.

Many localities sustain tourism through history museums. It may be in a place significant in the past for some event or activity or associated with an important historical figure. Or it may be something of a cultural warehouse where objects representative of the past are displayed in contemporary context. Where the built environment has been repeatedly modernized and the old thus largely stripped away, history museums offer aficionados of history some respite from present-day newness. Nonetheless, they offer highly fossilized cultural displays. Objects put behind glass or otherwise roped off from everyday living stand reified and even sacralized for their pastness. Certainly, I have perused my share of history museums. Indeed, I associate two life-informing experiences with one in particular: the Henry Ford Museum located outside Detroit in suburban Dearborn.

One cold, rainy October day in 1946, my mother, with a friend, took me there. We were, perhaps, the only visitors in the vast building, the museum essentially empty and very much our own private preserve. I was especially intrigued by the old cars and by an old gas station placed among them. The adults, on the other hand, liked the mock early-American street with its recreated blacksmith shop, cobbler's shop, and pharmacy, among other displays. Rather dull and boring, we all thought, were the hundreds of steam engines and thousands of farm implements that Henry Ford had especially valued in creating the place. Critics called the museum "Henry Ford's attic." A score of acres under one roof contained an extraordinary amount of old stuff, with very little interpretation. Ford realized that automobiles—especially cars for the masses, such as his Model T—would fundamentally change the nation. Indeed, automobility (cars and highways) did change the nation, likely more than any other technological development of the twentieth century. Ford set about to collect and thus preserve examples of the nation's pre-automobile past, especially the material culture of the rural Midwest he had known growing up on a farm in Dearborn. What I took away from that first visit was the realization that history can really matter.

In the early 1980s, I returned to the museum to attend a conference focused on the automobile's impact on the American experience, especially through the rise of highway travel. The museum had just installed a new exhibit that included a bigger, but not so very old, gas station, an old diner, part of a drive-in restaurant, a cabin from an old tourist court, and lots of old signs—the kinds that motorists would have seen along the nation's highways from the 1920s through the 1950s. And the vehicle collection was much enlarged to include trucks and buses and not just cars (Fig. 18). Gone was the old-fashioned street, most of the farm implements, and all but the largest of the stationary steam engines that Henry Ford had so relished. I spent much time wandering through the museum. It was crowded with numerous school groups and with parents and their children. Kids in various states of dress (and undress) pushed, shoved, and poked each other from one display to another: George Washington's field kit, the chair in which Abraham Lincoln had sat at Ford's Theater, the car in which John F. Kennedy was shot. Suddenly, it dawned on me that more than half of what I was seeing had been put up for display since I was a boy. Most of it was post-World War II in vintage. What now stood as "history" I had actually lived through. What's more, much of what was displayed were things that had fascinated me as a boy motoring with my parents across the Midwest. It was the stuff of the highway roadside. A few years later, I was invited to the Henry Ford Museum to help plan another new exhibit, one focused on highway-oriented tourism. The pigeon came home to roost, at least for a few days.[3]

Beyond museums, I had for years sought history in actual landscapes and places. I had done so not just in localities, such as Galena and Madison, where old buildings and indeed whole neighborhoods were undergoing restoration for touristic and other purposes. Rather, I had sought history everywhere, as if the whole world were a history museum. And I had done so almost always carrying a camera to record my discoveries. History is, after all, something that all of us actively live and make every day. Such was the principal message I sought to communicate to students in my classes. I used my photographs to illustrate nearly every aspect of every lecture. In teaching, I was concerned with helping students recognize and appreciate historical change, especially of the built environment. I was also anxious for them to comprehend the reasons for that change. Mine was not a celebration of progress. Much of the change that I witnessed and the change that I emphasized in class was, in my opinion, far from positive.

Born in 1939, I feel especially well positioned to assess change in terms of altered landscapes and places. The late-1940s were much like the late-1920s. As a child, I lived in a world of mom-and-pop grocery stores, locally owned and operated drugstores, specialty meat markets, shoe stores, and even hat shops. Streetcars and passenger trains were fundamental as to how I got around, although, admittedly, my family's automobiles loomed large indeed.

How could the motor car not be important to me? After all, I grew up in Detroit, the "Motor City." The 1950s were years of rapid change, and, indeed, much of it was change for change's sake. With savings built up during World War II and with higher take-home pay and increased hours of leisure, working people across the United States consumed goods and services as never before. And no longer did society's elites alone dictate tastes. A new popular culture came to the fore, suggestive of new ways of spending money and of using leisure time. Newness more fully displaced historicity in society's pantheon of cultural values. Detroit's auto makers introduced new models every year. Cars came to sport tail fins, which became increasingly exaggerated especially after Sputnik. And I was there to see it up close. Harley Earl, of General Motors, was in the driver's seat of style. And Steve, one of his sons, sat in the seat next to mine in seventh grade homeroom. Another friend's father worked for Chrysler; the tail fins of a Dodge were mounted on the wall of his bedroom, the brake lights constantly lit.

Living in Grosse Pointe, an area comprised of five small suburbs clustered along Lake St. Clair, was in itself instructive. Just looking out my bedroom window was informative (Fig. 19). Brought to view was a scene formed largely in the 1930s but also rooted as far back as the eighteenth century when French farm families tilled the soil. It was land bought up in the late nineteenth century by wealthy Detroiters seeking suburban escape from the nearby city. Along the lake were mansions built by families whose wealth came from lumbering, railroading, banking, and, of course, the manufacture of automobiles. Most Grosse Pointers, however, were part of an affluent middle class whose livelihoods derived from middle- to upper-middle-management positions in Detroit-based corporations. Already the big estates were being subdivided, and today there are but a handful left. A real estate market separate from Detroit's operated in "the Pointes," a market which, appropriately enough, involved a "point system." Private detectives, working for the realtors but paid by a so-called "property owners' association," filled out questionnaires on prospective house buyers, assigning points according to various social class and status attributes: race and ethnicity (including swarthiness), religion, education, occupation, nationality, club memberships, and even aspects of dress and speech (including grammar usage and dialect).[4] Applicants who did not accumulate enough points were steered elsewhere. Few residents knew of this, the scheme being discretely hidden from view. Then, in the early 1960s, a young minister got up in the pulpit to rate Christ using the realtors' system, and the cat was out of the bag. It was clear that Jesus would have been unable to buy a house in Grosse Pointe—he was unemployed, dark-complexioned, and Jewish.

Since I was not doing particularly well as a student, I was sent off to prep school: Culver Military Academy in Indiana. There I met the sons of fathers who owned oil companies, trucking companies, car dealerships, and outdoor advertising firms. I visited many of their homes. The father of one acquaintance was president of Goodyear. A very close friend was the grandson of Goodyear's founder, his father the president of Goodyear of Canada. Back in Grosse Pointe, a member of our church was quoted as saying, "What's good for General Motors is good for the country and vice versa."[5] The people who were making the decisions that actively pointed the nation toward dependence on the automobile were not strangers to me.

So comfortable was I with cars and with car people that it was assumed that, in college, I would complete a business degree and then work for a car company. When college graduation approached, I interviewed with several corporations. The recruiter from Ford complimented me. He said (without chuckling, straight-faced) that I was as impressive as any job candidate he had ever interviewed, but since there was a recession on the company was not hiring at the moment. Of course, my file would stay active, and they would contact me when the situation changed. When I got home that evening, there was already a form letter waiting for me from Ford. Essentially, it said: "Don't call us. We'll call you."

Along the way to completing an undergraduate degree in marketing I discovered academic geography. The idea that one could become a geographer and build a career around it was not alien to me, since an uncle by marriage—with a Ph.D. from the University of Chicago—had been one, ending his days as the geographer of the U.S. State Department. I went off to graduate school thinking about becoming an urban geographer and possibly establishing myself in urban planning. I was very much interested in cities: what they had once been like, how they varied, and how they were shaping up for the future.

Academic geography in the 1960s was undergoing tremendous change. Most human geographers—those who study culture's impact on landscape rather than nature's—were struggling to become social scientists, especially through the embrace of highly mathematical hypothesis-testing methods. Economic and urban geographers were especially intent on establishing a body of universally applicable generalizations, so as to understand (and, more importantly, to predict) how people locate themselves and their activities. Only by becoming scientists, it was asserted, might geographers truly command respect as scholars. Geographers, in other words, were to abstract away from the nitty-gritty of how people actually created, used, and otherwise experienced geography as landscape and place. No longer was there to be a place for the anecdotal or the merely descriptive, irrespective of the power of such to organize thought and action. To me, a discipline that neglected the meaningful stories around which people actually organize their lives was a discipline impoverished. How could geography, as an academic discipline, attract and hold the attention of non-geographers—lay people as well as other academics—if it diminished the import of peoples' direct experiencing of their surroundings?

The energy behind the "new" geography came mainly from the Midwest's larger universities, especially Chicago, Iowa, Michigan, Northwestern, and Ohio State. Perhaps such thinking suited a region organized in its maturity as both a producer of industrial raw material and a dedicated player in the nation's manufacturing economy. Midwestern landscapes and places tended to be highly utilitarian and, in their functionality, were susceptible to numerical modeling. For example, railroads radiated out of Chicago with smaller cities and towns of various sizes regularly spaced out along them, each place the focus of an appropriately-sized trade hinterland (Fig. 20).[1] How might such an urban pattern be modeled?

Something called "central place theory" was developed. It was not the only kind of spatial analysis used in understanding how and why urban places were sized and spaced as they were, but it was, perhaps, the most popular. Retail activities, for example, were seen to cluster in towns and cities in ordered fashion: larger places not only having more activity, but offering more variety vis-à-vis goods and services available. Urban places were seen to relate to one another in hierarchical arrangements. For example, only one large metropolis (Chicago) dominates the Midwest, with sets of cities (the St. Louis-sized places, the Peorias, the Terre Hautes) significantly smaller and more numerous progressively down the urban pyramid until the smallest category of town is reached. Size, it was found (all other things being equal), was related to geographical location—the smallest town and city hinterlands nesting neatly within the hinterlands of progressively larger places.

Land use in Midwestern towns and cities also seemed to invite numerical analysis. Such variables as parcel size, distance from city center (or other location), and land values could all be analyzed quantitatively. Most Midwestern towns were structured very much alike, as Theodore Dreiser surmised. First, there was a grid of streets, one of which was a main commercial avenue intersecting or paralleling a railroad (Fig. 21). Outward were mainly residential streets punctuated by churches, schools, and the like. In cities, land use was far more complex, but it could still be generalized in terms of concentric rings of growth over time, sectors of development oriented to lines of transportation, or clusters of activity mutually reinforced in some way (Fig. 22).

The Midwest's rural landscapes also seemingly invited quantitative analysis. Land was surveyed with geometric regularity, divided by township and range lines into one-square-mile sections. Roads in most parts of the Midwest came to conform to these boundaries, meeting at right angles oriented to the cardinal directions. Such regularity reflected an embrace of the Enlightenment's penchant for order—the search for order being the motivating force, of course, behind science. It also reflected the avid pursuit of capitalism's drive for profit. Entrepreneurs drove change through cycles of investment, disinvestment, and reinvestment—behavior, many geographers argued, that could and should also be quantitatively analyzed from spatial points of view.

Scientism in geography intrigued me, but I remained too much a historian at heart. I remained wed more to humanistic approaches to understanding, those that emphasize the cultural and social values that influence human behavior. Quantification was fine, but why should geographers limit themselves, as more and more did, to variables—things—that could be counted? Besides, the new theories, with their mathematical models, did not relate well with what I knew about geographical decision-making: ground-level explanations of how cities, for example, changed and why.

Near where I lived in Grosse Pointe, construction of the new Edsel Ford Expressway had destroyed Harper Avenue, the principal commercial strip in Detroit's East Side suburb of Harper Woods. The route was substantially influenced by the political skills of a friend's father, a vice president at J. L. Hudson, who served on a vital highway commission. Thu expressway's routing eliminated much of Hudson's retail competition.[2] In another up-close experience, one of my father's clients—a vice president at General Motors—explained how it was that the company's new Technical Center came to be located in suburban Warren. He named the officers at GM who had speculated in real estate there. By successfully lobbying local government for road and utility improvements, they made the corporation's move into Warren seem imperative.

In my opinion, geographers practicing spatial analysis were not coming to grips with issues of social empowerment. In retrospect, their analyses were highly simplistic, certainly in terms of underlying intellectualization. Things were seen to be distributed geographically in response to anonymous social forces—general tendencies understood as operating across a population but not necessarily in response to specific decision-making. Gross assumptions were introduced: for example, business people sought always to maximize profit and minimize loss, and they were usually successful in doing so. It seemed to me that real explanation lay in telling stories that wove together the many strands of human intentionality, not just those aspects of life that could be conveniently analyzed statistically. General Motors and J. L. Hudson were profit-making entities, but decision-making as to where activities ought and ought not be located did not necessarily favor a "theoretically optimal" location, the principal guiding assumption that underlay most spatial analysis. Life—and business—were more complex than that.

Whereas spatial analysis embraced short-term change in the search for process-oriented explanation, it was largely confined to contemporary timelines for which quantitative data, already gathered (and, indeed, already aggregated by geographical area) was readily available.

By the 1970s, researchers had only to order computer tapes from a range of private and public agencies, load the relevant data, and "crunch it" (as it was popularly termed), using one standard analytical routine or another. Concern with the distant past was nil, in part due to a general lack of quantified historical data, let alone data conveniently codified. I, on the other hand, had become quite interested in the distant past, with my curiosity focused more and more on aspects of life that had never been enumerated. Perhaps like a detective or a lawyer building a case for litigation, I found myself dependent upon highly fragmented historical evidence, clues to human intentionality and behavior that required more than a little extrapolation. The distant past was something one had to acculturate to, rather like an area specialist preparing to leave home for overseas. Indeed, the past, even the Midwestern past, is for today's Americans much like a foreign country. The historian's task was to put his or her evidence carefully into context so that cogent stories might be told.

After earning a business degree at Western Michigan University and a master's in geography at Southern Illinois University, I completed a Ph.D. at Indiana University. My dissertation focused on the influence of salt, a resource important in the early settlement of the trans-Appalachian West.[3] It was a giant step away from my city-oriented interests that had been largely contemporary in orientation. I took the plunge and became a historical geographer—something of a scholarly time-traveler. My work focused on how the Ohio River had once tied together the "Ohio Valley," a regional concept in use before the term "Midwest" was conceived (Fig. 23). Some of my data came from diaries and travel narratives written by actual movers and shakers, but most of the narratives I examined were written by those who were merely passing through. They were primarily journalists who wrote for audiences in the East or in Europe, and, besides selling books, they came to investigate, evaluate, and advise others as to settlement opportunities on the then-Western frontier.

Eventually, I refocused on early twentieth-century travel description. I turned to studying the impact of the automobile not only on past landscape, but also on what people in the past experienced of landscape and place. By so reorienting, however, I found myself at the margins of historical geographical scholarship. Historical geographers, along with those who called themselves cultural geographers, resisted human geography's penchant for scientism by embracing the humanistic orientations of other academic disciplines, such as history and cultural anthropology. With that I remained in full sympathy. But, even today, most historical geographers continue to focus on the eighteenth and nineteenth centuries, relatively few being interested in the twentieth century, let alone the twenty-first. Additionally, they mainly revisit the great ideas and controversies of academic history rather than explore issues more clearly geographical, such as travel. In other words, very few are interested in the automobile and what it has meant for life in America. Only recently have most cultural geographers, for their part, moved beyond preoccupation with rural folk cultures.

Ever since James Agee coined the word "roadside" in a 1934 *Fortune* article, the term has generally been understood to describe commercial strip development both within and peripheral to cities and towns. It alludes to the rise of automobile convenience, whereby goods and services are readily accessed by customers arriving to shop by car (Fig. 24). Agee described this new geographical reality with just a bit of hyperbole. The roadside, he wrote, was "incomparably the most hugely extensive market the human race [had] ever set up to tease and tempt and take money from the human race." Already in the United States, he reported, roadside selling was generating more than $3 billion in sales.[4] Nonetheless, geographers then, as now, remained largely unconcerned.[5]

This relative neglect has come despite the fact that retailing in the nation is now nearly totally automobile-convenient. People motor to shop, expecting parking to be close at hand. Purchases made over the

Internet or by phone are conveniently delivered to the door by truck. Additionally, one finds today's new residential subdivisions, office and industrial parks, and, indeed, all manner of development flung out along, and largely accessible only from, auto thoroughfares. Urban geographers, still focused on contemporary processes of change, have been steadily at work researching and teaching about continuing urban decentralization in the United States, but they have stuck with geography's spatial analytical approach, choosing to emphasize broad patterns of short-term land-use change and population shifts. They have generally ignored what Americans specifically see and react to in auto-oriented landscapes and places. They do not focus at the scale of the American roadside.[6]

Geographers are wed to using maps. Relatively few embrace photography, whether of their own making or that of others. By using photography extensively in the classroom, I sought to instill in students a predisposition to look at and speculate about the ordinary world around them, down to and including the architecture of the roadside. What are the important similarities from place to place? What are the important differences? In what ways do some landscapes and places, in the Midwest, for example, stand as truly distinctive (Fig. 25)? These questions put me more in line with cultural geographers, who saw in the built environment a kind of archive of regional variation. Firsthand field observation invited camera use not only as a means of recording what was there, but also as a means of orienting to it. Most cultural geographers, however—as do geographers in general—think about geography mainly in map analogs.[7] In reducing the three-dimensional world to a flat, two-dimensional surface, map projections involve mathematical abstraction, in and of itself an invitation to generalization. Thematic maps, the basis of much geographical analysis, abstract the world further through focus on limited topics (such as demographics and land use) and use of data aggregated by area or location. In contrast to maps, photographs tend to excite interest in detail. One can see people and things at the scale of an actual landscape or place. Photos are decidedly descriptive rather than analytical, although they can be analyzed for what they portray and for underlying purpose. What was the photographer trying to show? Why was the photo made? Who, in other words, constituted the intended audience? Photos of landscape suggest what it is that one can see (or once could have seen) in a place. They also suggest, especially through compositional emphasis, how those things ought to be visualized. Visualization is of fundamental import when it comes to understanding how people make and use places.[8]

Professional geography has always thrived in the Midwest. During the 1970s, the majority of the nation's practicing geographers worked in the region—in teaching, planning, and market research, among other occupations. But, in recent decades, departments of geography have been eliminated at the University of Michigan, Northwestern University, and even the University of Chicago, the latter department long considered the discipline's flagship program. What happened? In part, a "follow-the-leader" syndrome operated after Harvard, Stanford, and Yale earlier eliminated their geography programs. This begs the question for which I should like to propose a hypothesis. Perhaps there was something more fundamental. Might it have been the new geography? Did geographers inadvertently throw out the baby with the bath water? Perhaps the discipline became too abstract in its intentions, removing itself too far from people's meaningful everyday experiencing? Many university administrators concluded that spatial modeling, promising as it might be, ought, nonetheless, to be pursued within topically oriented disciplines—for example, geology as the study of the earth's crust or economics as the study of society's production, distribution, and consumption of wealth. Location, many thought, was an insufficient concern to justify separate departmental organization.

As a professor of geography at a large Midwestern university, I was constantly challenged, both in professional and social situations, to define and defend my discipline (Fig. 26). The University of Illinois at

Urbana-Champaign is dominated by engineering (including computing) and the hard sciences. Agriculture, the institution's original rationale, is today energized principally by bio-engineering or genomic research. Geography was simply not something with which most of my colleagues in the university could readily identify. "You mean you actually do research?" a colleague once asked. The new theory-based geography was, perhaps, simply too new, its promise too far from being fulfilled. And the older, more descriptive sort of regional study, at least so far as geographers had earlier practiced it, was not sufficiently sophisticated.

Questions of location or areal distribution nest well down many a scholar's intellectual ladder of concern. For many, location is at best a third order of questioning. In the organization of knowledge, focus is first on the subject matter or topic, a "what" question. Geographers may claim to study "space" or things located in space. But this does not seem to answer that question, since, to many minds, space merely implies a vacuum, a nothingness. A second order of knowing involves change over time, a "when" question. Very important is the understanding of change. Indeed, explanation traditionally has hinged on understanding process, the manner by which things change. Only third comes the issue of location, the "where" question. Few scholars claim that location and spatial arrangement are totally unimportant in life, but many argue that questions of location are best handled by those focused either on subject matter or change. They see location merely as an effect (or a result) and not as a fundamental cause. Academic disciplines, such thinking asserts, ought to be focused on "causes" and not "effects." This thinking overlooks the fact that location both influences and is influenced by the social, political, and economic aspects of life. In the conduct of everyday life, location is both a cause and an effect.

Might academic geography have been better served if, during the 1960s, geographers, including those in the Midwest, had remained dedicated to traditional geographical concepts, especially the concept of "place" (Fig. 27)? Places can be thought of as existing relative to one another in map-like two-dimensional space. But that is just one important spatial implication. Places are also bounded, sometimes physically with walls, a floor, and a ceiling in three dimensions. They have entrances and exits. Places also exist in time, opening and closing in daily, weekly, and annual cycles. They function for set durations. Places can be characterized by the normal activities in them, and by the people (or kinds of people) who normally engage in those activities. Additionally, places can be characterized by the props or furnishings regularly employed as people interact with one another. Places defined at different scales variously relate to one another, sometimes in hierarchical manner.

Place, in all its many facets and not just mere location, deserves the human geographer's focus. All life "takes place," it is often said. Fully understanding human behavior requires an understanding of how people create and use places, what geographers now refer to as "human spatiality."[9] Every action or event is situated (or embedded) in a spatial relationship. Thus, places are constructed by and help construct social relations. Society cannot be fully understood without taking both aspects into consideration.

I also wonder if academic geography might have fared better had emphasis on the firsthand experiencing of places been retained. Geographical scholarship was, after all, substantially the outgrowth of early exploration. Adventurers, who trekked into the unknown, returned to write up their impressions, and a distinctive geographical literature was born. It was through direct observation ("in the field," if you will) that the geographical outlines of the world became known. But, in the 1960s, field-oriented education, at least in human geography, dropped by the bye as economic, urban, and other geographers acquainted themselves with the mysteries of quantification, first with calculators and then with computers. I went through two graduate degrees without any field experience. What I learned about the world outside the classroom, the library, or the computer lab came largely through my own initiative and largely on weekend jaunts with my wife and young daughters. Such personal exploration served to validate, if not energize, more formal courses of study. Take for example, my getting to know a cousin's farm at Panther's Den, in the Shawnee Ozark Hills of southern Illinois.

Family lore says that the farm was won in a poker game. When I first saw it as a child, an elderly tenant, with his two mules and several dogs, lived a solitary life there. He grew a few acres of corn and hunted for a living. What impressed me most from that first visit was the wildcat skin nailed to the chicken coop, the animal having been shot only the night before. Some twenty years later, the tenant was long dead, and everything, including the access road to the farm, lay in a state of abandonment. Accessing the "Den," a narrow cleft in a steep rock escarpment, required a mile-long walk through dense brush, swatting at mosquitos. One visit stands out as especially memorable. Walking in parallel with us, and clearly trespassing, was an elderly man accompanied by his son-in-law, as we learned. He had been born on the neighboring farm shortly after his father, a Confederate veteran of the Civil War, brought his family from Tennessee to homestead in Illinois. No reading of the census record could have revealed what we learned about pioneer settlement that afternoon. No statistical analysis could have equaled its emotive power.

Farming the thin soils in and around Panther's Den had been difficult. Our elderly companion told us that he, as a child, trudged up and down the escarpment several times a day, carrying water for household use. He wanted to see the spring at Panther's Den one last time, he said. Here was a place etched in his memory: a place of life-informing experience. At the spring, hidden under an overhang of rock, with its flow of water down to a mere trickle, we sat for an hour talking about how life had been lived eighty years earlier. Today, forty years further along, Panther's Den is part of the Shawnee National Forest. It is a much sought-out destination for hikers as well as for people coming in on horseback. And the area is now totally reforested. Coyotes howl at night. The gray wolf is once more common. Place, with all of its emotional and intellectual attachments, is what human geography, I think, should be about. Focus on the meaning of places can serve to integrate various kinds of knowing (the what, when, and where questions combined). Sometimes it can do so most forcefully, as I learned that afternoon.

Might academic geography have been better served if greater concern had been given to excellence in writing as well? Might emphasis on words rather than numbers have been more productive? In graduate school, I was instructed always to write in a neutral voice void of all emotion, thus to assume the pose of a fully objective observer. Scientism in geography has rarely produced great writing: communication as impelling as it is convincing. Instead, it has wrought a kind of blandness. Perhaps it was a Midwestern-inspired penchant for functionality (the prizing of the utilitarian so strong across the region) that diverted the field's practitioners from creative writing to mere reporting? Perhaps it was the typical Midwesterner's preference for plain talk?

Until recently, many geographers have been guilty of asking very significant questions, but questions, nonetheless, for which they lacked an ability to answer or answer fully—questions, for example, about environmental change at the global scale. Sufficiently sophisticated tools of analysis were simply unavailable. But in the computerized age, and especially through use of GIS (geographical information systems) technology, today's physical geographers can answer many of those questions and answer them well. The promise of the new geography of the 1960s, with its emphasis on spatial analysis, may yet be fulfilled as human geographers use GIS to interpret land-use change, at both local and global scales. Luckily, most of the Midwest's universities retained their geography departments, programs now substantially reenergized through GIS. To be convincing, however, geographers—whatever their other competencies and wherever they work—must write well. And even the most sophisticated of GIS images require solid "ground truth," obtainable only through direct field observation.

It was an outsider, John Brinckerhoff Jackson (better known as J. B. Jackson), who incited many historical and cultural geographers not only to think of geography's literary potential, but to do so in terms of what he called "landscape studies." Jackson defined "landscape" as "more than an area of attractive rural or natural scenery. It is a space or a collection of spaces made by a group of people who modify the natural environment to survive, to create order, and to produce a just and lasting society."[10] As such, landscapes surround even as they contain. Jackson's thinking also stimulated scholarly interest in the concept of "place," which he treated, quite simply, as centers of human concern and activity. Jackson emphasized the need to get out and look at everyday places, not through the lens of a satellite positioned high above the earth's surface but at or near ground level, as one normally experiences the world. Jackson stressed the need to talk to people about what landscapes and places mean. Founder of an influential magazine, *Landscape* (1951–1968), J. B. Jackson certainly influenced my becoming a human geographer. He also led me off in the direction of interdisciplinary teaching and research involvements. Jackson, who taught both at Harvard and the University of California at Berkeley, also impacted the thinking of architects, landscape architects, urban planners, and, significantly, photographers, convincing them of the importance of common, everyday places in human life. He encouraged scholars and designers alike to examine the cultural values implicit in the making of, the regulation of, and the use of places.[11]

J. B. Jackson was greatly influenced by Carl O. Sauer, one of the principal figures in the early evolution of both historical and cultural geography in the United States. Sauer's emphasis was on "reading" landscapes for meaning, especially the social symbolism of material culture.[12] Today, many cultural geographers, taking their lead from social theorists, focus on interpreting the ideological implications of landscape and place. They seek to understand the "power relations" of different kinds of people in various kinds of places.[13] Many have come to emphasize the representation of landscape and place over material actualities. For them, analyzing the content of written narrative, cartography, or visual art, including photographs, offers a means of understanding the values that underlie people's place-oriented behaviors.[14] I certainly concur with this approach. Even renowned critics, such as Chicagoan David Brooks, columnist of *The New York Times*, have become enamored with the importance of human geography in understanding our place in the world. And the great novelist Jim Harrison, who was born and raised in Michigan and whose writings are immersed in the landscape, has written: ". . . inside the relatively new acdemic discipline of human geography our sameness is diminished by our differences."[15]

Today, human and cultural geography is practiced more on the nation's coasts—both east and west—and in the South, as opposed to the Midwest. I can only speculate as to why this might be. Undoubtedly, it has to do with the vigorous expansion of the geography departments, as well as the foreign studies programs, in many of the nation's state universities—universities that are being energized through boisterous regional economic growth. It is also a function of healthy regional studies programs focused not abroad but very much on the domestic scene: centers for the study of Appalachia, New England, the South, the Southwest, and the West, for example. Only a few Midwestern universities support anything approaching Midwest studies. And those programs (Great Plains Studies at the University of Nebraska at Lincoln or Great Lakes Studies at Wayne State University in Detroit, for example) do not embrace the Midwest in its entirety. Perhaps the Midwest is simply too mainstream in the American experience, and seemingly too transparent accordingly, to warrant such attention. What is missing, historian Andrew Cayton observed, is the absence of contested regional meaning, thus providing relatively little discourse about what the Midwest means among both scholars and popular commentators.[16]

The Midwest has been many things to me. It is where my family's roots run deep. I have lived only one year of my life in another section of the nation (the year I taught at the University of Maine at Orono). The Midwest is where I chose to pursue an academic career. It is a place I have grown to admire and enjoy. I like the Midwest's open spaces. When I travel, particularly in the American Northeast or in Europe, I find myself getting claustrophobic. Things seem to close in on me. Is it the traffic? Or the density of buildings (even outside of cities)? Or the confinement of hill and valley? Is it the shadow of seemingly ever-present tree canopies? Living in central Illinois, I have come to appreciate flat landscapes with far horizons. Mine are panoramic landscapes where the sky, with its constantly shifting light, figures prominently. I relish lots of elbow room. Seasonally, central Illinois blooms like a garden (Fig. 28). There is something about having farms and farmers close at hand (Fig. 29).

Champaign-Urbana, where I live, is a modern city that works. It functions marvelously well, reflecting, in part, its newness. The oldest building in Champaign dates only from the mid-1850s. Nonetheless, there is still sufficient time-depth to keep any historical geographer busy and enough social diversity to keep any cultural geographer happy. And there are miles and miles of highway for those focused on the roadside. Like the Midwest's other smaller cities, Champaign-Urbana is easy to get around in. And yet, being a university town, it contains most of the services and cultural opportunities that people in much larger places esteem. And, should I want to get away, I am but a day's drive (a long day's drive, admittedly) from Atlanta, Dallas, New Orleans, Philadelphia, or Toronto. I am in the middle of it all.

I feel a certain pride coming from a region traditionally so important to the nation and the world economically. True, Midwesterners have never fully controlled their own economic destinies. The Midwest has always looked to New York City or to Washington, D.C., for direction and, more recently, to Los Angeles for what might be called inspiration. Nineteenth-century investment capital came largely from the East. It was money used to speculate in land, create farms, sink mines, build railroads, lay out towns and cities, and, of course, make things such as farm implements and cars. In return, the mid-continent came to produce most of the nation's wheat, meat, iron, coal, and, early on, its oil—the resources that drove the American nation's industrialization. From the Midwest's farms and small towns ventured many of the people who made New York City and Washington, D.C., important. They were people who made the country run and even kept it together—people with names such as Rockefeller and Lincoln.

Today, however, the nation looks to both its east and west coasts for economic, if not cultural, direction. The Pacific Coast is now especially ascendant, if only as an economic hinge to booming Asia. But what the nation eats and what the nation thinks still resonates with clear Midwestern implication, whether it is test marketing new products in Columbus, Ohio, or testing political leanings in Peoria, Illinois. The nation still drives cars made in Detroit, although Detroit and other cities, such as Terre Haute, struggle to redefine themselves as something other than "Rust Belt." The Midwest is a region still very much evolving.

Chicago is no longer the nation's "second city," and Chicagoans do not own or control the city's largest banks as previously. But the city is still the commodity marketer to the world. It is a city remarkably well-preserved in many of its older sections, so one can get a real sense of history there as well as a glimpse of the future. I have watched over the years the effects of racial discrimination play out in the redlining of banks, the steering and blockbusting of realty agents, the ravages of underemployment and unemployment, and the rise of a drug culture and related criminality.[1] Chicago, as other cities, has suffered from the effects of "white flight," as affluent inner-city people, most of them white, flocked to suburban "safety." Today, however, a building boom in the central city is underway. It very much follows the geographical templates of traditional mass transit, promising high-population densities and abundant street life for the future. The city is re-energized by a post-industrial economic resurgence, especially in the form of downtown white-collar jobs.

Although I am a city boy suburban-bred, since coming to Illinois I have tried to keep myself acquainted with the Midwest's changing farms and small towns. In my locality, I have followed the growth and impact of big agribusinesses and the acceleration of farm consolidation influenced by increased specialization in "cash grain." In my area, each technological or market shift readily reflects in the tearing down of old buildings (once they are amortized) and sometimes, but not always, in their replacement with the new. And yet old values persist. Substantially is farmland owned, leased, or otherwise held under the stewardship of farm families of German or Scandinavian origins—the land valued as patrimony to be passed generation to generation. This is especially true of groups such as the Old Order Amish (Fig. 30).

Within an hour's drive are several areas fully dominated by German-Americans, each area constituting a kind of American "Germania." Everywhere landscape is neat and orderly—not only the farms, but also the small towns where main streets are very much alive, supported by surrounding farm populations networked as a close community through church congregation (Fig. 31). Of course, I can also find towns withering away, where local retailing, the schools, and even the churches have floundered over recent decades. They survive as little more than bed-room places and many as little more than rural ghettoes where society's impoverished and dispossessed languish as surely as in many deprived inner-city neighborhoods.[2] The American Midwest is a highly urbanized region, and yet parts of it remain relatively unpopulated and undevel-oped: extensive portions of northern Michigan, Wisconsin, and Min-nesota and much of the reforested hill country of southern Ohio, southern Indiana, southern Illinois, and the Ozarks of Missouri.

Unfortunately, with a wife and family of my own, visits home to sub-urban Detroit left little time to experience all areas of Michigan. In recent summers, however, we have rented cottages on the Lake Michi-gan shore (Fig. 32). It is a central location to which our Pennsylvania and Nebraska daughters and their families can come for annual gather-ings. As a child, I accompanied my parents frequently to such resorts as Mackinac Island's Grand Hotel in Michigan's Upper Peninsula. Rarely did we get off the main highways, mainly because most of north-ern Michigan's "cut-over" land was so ugly, lumbering having left little more than scrub forest over extensive areas. A half-century later, matur-ing forest greets the eye, and northern Michigan is attractive once again. And the "fruit belt" along the Lake Michigan shore is booming, not only from market gardening, but from a flourishing resort industry.

"I'll save Wisconsin for retirement," I always said when planning sum-mer trips. Having recently retired from teaching, I have begun exploring it again. Dairying, not cash grain, dominates the state's rural economy, and I am still learning about farm life tied to the routines of cows rather than to the growing cycles of corn and soybeans. Today, families with German or Scandinavian roots fully dominate farming in the Badger State (Fig. 33). In Minnesota, Duluth and the Lake Superior shore northeast of that fascinating city have attracted me two summers running in recent years (Fig. 34). Duluth was a city built around the shipping of grain and iron ore. Spreading up, over, and beyond the steep hillside that overlooks the harbor, today's city contains a wealth of historic architecture. Growing up beside Lake St. Clair, I was fully aware of Duluth. I was enamored of the lake freighters that carried iron ore and wheat southward from that place and coal in return. With the economic boom of the 1950s, shipping companies put into service almost everything that would float. On summer afternoons lines of boats coming and going were ever-present on Lake St. Clair, stretching from horizon to horizon.

I am slowly getting to know the Great Plains better. My earliest travels across the plains were by train and, therefore, at night. Railroad passengers, it was assumed, would see little of interest across the flat prairies and plains west of Chicago. They might as well be asleep. For most Americans, the Great Plains is still very much an area to "get across." And so it was for me, I am sorry to admit, even when I traveled by car in recent decades. Only now am I directing travel to Kansas, Nebraska, and the Dakotas as places of destination. Farming, at least traditional family farming, is very much in decline across the drier parts of those states. Much of the land has been removed from cultivation. Land still under cultivation has been consolidated into giant farm operations. As rural population declined, the area's small towns (its "central places") declined as well. Many of the smallest towns have virtually disappeared (Fig. 35).

My firsthand exposure to the Midwest has been selective, and it is still incomplete. The Midwest is a big place, some 703,000 square miles. It would be impossible for anyone to see it all, even superficially, let alone to feel fully rooted everywhere. But, it is against the Midwest that I do know—the Midwestern background that is mine— that I take the measure of who I am, what I have been doing with my life, and where that might yet lead. To do so gives me a sense of being not only anchored, but well-directed. It may be self-delusion, but that is how I feel. As well, there is something fundamentally satisfying about pursuing scholarly interests first cultivated in childhood. This seems especially true in terms of my travels—my early trip-taking was very much regional in scope.

In a setting far from *Hoosier Holiday*, in a book concerning his jaunts in and around New York City, Theodore Dreiser asserted: "The beauty of life is involved very largely with the outline of its scenery."[3] His assertion sticks in my mind as something of importance. Of course, one needs to get below the surface of scenery in assessing landscape and place, as in assessing life generally. Nonetheless, his words suggest a certain line of thought: for me, life is substantially attended to through the visual outlines of landscape and the visual details of place.[4] Our surroundings are filled with "to whom it may concern" messages waiting to be read. In the process of their decipherment, beauty is frequently revealed. If not beauty, then often truth. Important are the messages of landscape and place that resonate in deeply personal ways. Yet the most important, I would argue, are those that not only excite individually, but collectively—the messages that resonate strongly with countless people.

Cultural or social implication (shared memory rather than the merely personal) truly legitimizes scholarly endeavors focused on landscape and place. One asks not only what the Midwest means to me, but what that meaning might mean collectively. Two stances are required: concern with what has made the Midwest distinctive unto itself and concern with what the region has held in common with other areas. It is probably the latter line of questioning that might best be encouraged. The idea of the Midwest incorporates many themes basic to the American experience. Out of the Midwest have come images that speak forcefully of values fundamental to what many Americans consider their nation to be: a place for opportunity for economic self-aggrandizement, freedom to assert oneself through communities of mutual support, and the ability to reposition oneself socially.

The American success story is substantially rooted in the Midwest. Perhaps that is the most differentiating thing about the region's history. Despite the discrimination practiced there, the region offered, as it continues to offer today, opportunity to a diverse population. The frontier experience, as celebrated in the writing of American history, was largely forged in what became the Midwest. A large portion of the mid-continent's climate, soil, and topography were found to be unsurpassed for farming. In the nineteenth century, land was liberally made available in ways that sustained family enterprise and, more importantly, generated a supply of free labor highly motivated and technically accomplished. Abundance through mechanized agriculture, complemented by mining, lumbering, and other extractive enterprises, in turn, stimulated rapid urban growth: the region's cities, as its farms and small towns, becoming magnets to migrants from great distances, capital for development coming from afar as well. Perhaps Americans ought to remember the Midwest as a kind of metaphoric middle ground: a place of passage where many American ideals were worked out.

For those who have roots in the region, the Midwest ought to carry personal charge of strong geographical implication: what some geographers call a "sense of place." Sense of place, it seems to me, is fully related to what some historians call "historical memory." At play are sets of stories that people tell one another in explaining who they are. These are stories that necessarily involve remembered landscapes and places as experienced at particular points in time. When memories about place are widely shared, they stand as a kind of cultural imperative, so that even the most ordinary of places can come to seem extraordinary. Such places, as historian Hasia Diner noted, "become transformed into spaces throbbing with meaning."[5]

Of course, different people come to those meanings differently. I began to look at the Midwest through a train window, and then the window of a car, a small boy challenged to make sense out of what he saw. I did so by relating what I saw with past family connections. And I continue to do so today, augmenting those impressions with the experience of my own living and working in the region. As a scholar, I became preoccupied with the study of landscapes as they contained places variously constituted. I came to view landscape as a kind of archive where historical and geographical facts otherwise poorly recorded, or not recorded at all, might be gathered and assessed. And I still do. But I value landscape more than ever not only for what it encourages people to remember, but also for what it encourages people to feel—and feel strongly.

Late in life, I may have become a revisionist. It occurs to me that the term "Midwest" may no longer be the most appropriate regional label, although I would actually hate to give it up. Might the rubric "Midlands," or maybe "Middle America," better serve? Geographically, the region remains in the middle of it all, but is no longer "western" as we have come to variously use that term. These days, Midwesterners tend to be characterized socially as occupying a kind of middle ground. It is a Will-it-play-in-Peoria? sort of thing. Implied, perhaps, is a conservative worldview that would isolate America if taken to the extreme, something that would turn the nation in on itself, thus to make everyone a conformist.

Midwestern politics, on the other hand, has traditionally been progressive and variously given to reform. Egalitarian ideals may have played out with leveling influence, even to the point of enforcing conformity, for example in the region's small towns as Sinclair Lewis reminded. But Midwestern cities, including Peoria, have historically been places of confrontation quite contrary to mindless middle-of-the-road homogeneity, political or otherwise. In the cities, sentimental reform and its small-town-inspired idealizing of democratic harmony, was joined by oppositional reform, especially labor's critique of corporate capitalism. Out of an urban Midwest in the twentieth century came direct democracy (direct primaries, citizen initiative, the recall referendum, and restrictions on lobbying), corporate regulation (of rail-roads, grain elevators, banks, and insurance companies), and health and safety advocacy (factory and mine safety laws, pure food and drug legislation, workman's compensation laws, and protective legislation for women and children).[1] Given the propagation of such values, I do not think it true that Midwesterners, in the words of one historian, have nurtured "a culture of the lowest common denominator, a way of life based on highlighting what people share, rather than the myriad ways in which they are diverse."[2] If the Midwest is politically middle-of-the-road, it may be because its people have pulled the rest of the nation in around them.

As historian Kathleen Conzen observed, scholarship on American regions traditionally focused on objectively identifying characteristics (such as social and physical attributes) that are common to a geographi-cal area but uncommon elsewhere. Using such a method, the Midwest, as a place exclusively possessing distinctive characteristics fully unto itself, has been very hard to find.[3] Americans may think they know where it is but still remain unsure as to what it is. Today, the thrust toward strict objectivity in regional analysis has shifted toward greater subjectivity.

"Regions are now seen as human constructions rather than expressions of an immutable reality created from objective conditions of place and space," argued Jon Gjerde in his discussion of the Midwest's "middleness."[4] The new focus compels scholars to take into considera-tion how people think and act. The alternative and complementary iden-tities that individuals, including scholars, bring to discussing the Midwest as a region are a large part of what defines the region. In this view, making sense of a region is fundamentally a backward-looking exercise fully inviting to autobiography.[5] It is, indeed, a matter of prob-ing the Midwest in the popular imagination.

As I learned as four-year-old child fascinated by my first motor trip into open country, things change and evolve. The world is not a set piece. However, not only do things change, but thinking changes and evolves also. The idea of the Midwest (call it the Midlands or Middle America, if you will) constantly begs reassessment, not just in a personal sense, but, more importantly, in a communal sense: the Midwest reassessed as widely shared thinking freighted with ever-shifting cultural, economic, political, and social meanings. That is why looking at and thinking about Midwestern landscapes and places continues to fascinate me. I play a never-ending game. It is not just what I see and think; it is also what other people see and think. What do the evidences of landscape and place suggest? What, in other words, does the Midwest's geography tell us? There is nothing like taking a day off, getting in a car, and driving off to contemplate such things. I always finding it edifying, even when (perhaps especially) the ground covered is long familiar.

I drove down to Terre Haute the other day. The Terre Haute House, the hotel where I used to stay with my parents, was being torn down. A photo or two of the demolition, I thought, might be nice to have. Ordinarily, it would have taken less than two hours to get there, but, leaving at daybreak, it was well into the afternoon before I arrived. The first snowfall of the season had given the area a pleasing winter aspect. Farm fields, for example, stood etched in snow—ridge and furrow amplified in striking patterns of black and white, another impelling reason to carry a camera. Tied to classroom teaching over the years, too seldom had I ventured out specifically to photograph winter landscapes. One might think from looking at my photographs that the Midwest is primarily a sunny, summer place. Here was opportunity to make amends. Snow squalls slowed the commuters then streaming into Champaign-Urbana. It was not the sort of day that a normal person might choose to leave the comforts of home. It was cloudy and promised to be dark and gray all day. The temperature was well below freezing. But I have found that travel is usually well rewarded when pursued in ways and, at times, beyond the normal. The same might also be said about scholarship.

I chose to avoid main highways by wandering the narrow back roads, zig-zagging across the area's section-line grid. Always on the horizon was the outline of a distant grain elevator marking one or another town, places to be briefly reconnoitered in passing through. Although I have been a diligent explorer in my locality for some forty years, there still remains much to discover. For one thing, I am constantly adopting new topical enthusiasms and, thus, constantly coming to appreciate things in a landscape previously ignored. For another, there are so many miles of road to explore (more than a thousand miles in Champaign County alone). Of course, it is helpful to motor without urgency and with a mindset that says stopping frequently is okay. By pausing in a place, one allows a landscape to sink in more fully: not just through the eyes, but through all the senses. One learns to recognize opportunity which involves seizing the unexpected. A landscape does not shout out its meanings; rather, understandings require teasing out through careful, if not caring, examination.

Take, for example, one farmstead that I encountered after an hour or so of driving. Coming around a sharp curve, I almost passed it without noticing. It was located in a grove of trees along what was originally the edge of a tall-grass prairie. Why stop? First, I thought it likely to be an early settlement site. The area's oldest farmsteads tended to "edge-of-grove" locations where settlers, beginning in the 1830s, used wooden plows to break the light forest soils. Cultivating out on the grasslands came much later, once the land had been drained and, more importantly, once heavy steel plows, capable of cutting through the deep-rooted prairie grass, were introduced. Second, I could see an accumulation of barns, cribs, and other buildings that suggested a century or more of farm activity. Old things had not been torn down. Or thrown out. An old windmill, still operating, clattered in the wind. There was even an old night pasture where plow horses would have been kept. An open door in a machine shed brought to view an array of vintage tractors. This was a place once doted upon with much affection. Someone had found contentment here. Then it had all abruptly ended. The farm house, victim to fire, was completely fallen into its basement, a charred ruin beyond redemption. A dream had turned into a nightmare. The place had not been occupied for years.

Downtown Terre Haute, once I got there, also seemed filled with broken dreams but promise for the future also. Where US 40 and US 41 once crossed—the intersection of Wabash Avenue and Seventh Street, what locals still call "the Crossroads of America"—I found the Terre Haute House, much reduced to rubble. A wrecking ball swung overhead, suspended from a giant crane. Carried away to storage were the pillars that once guarded the hotel's main entrance. They would be, I was told, reused in constructing two new motor hotels on the site. Tradition was to be carried forward. Recorded history said that, at this location, there had always been a hotel, starting with the Prairie House, built in the 1840s at what was then the edge of town. Now a former coal operator, turned real estate developer, was undertaking to renew historical memory and, perhaps, a sense of place. Of course, he was tearing down what many people had long considered the city's most important landmark.

But why not? The decision was not irrational. The existing building, vacant for more than three decades, was fully derelict. It made business sense to start anew. Return on capital, one need not be reminded, is truly the business of the Midwest. It is what drives the region's utilitarian character, its ever-emergent functionality. Much of Terre Haute's traditional downtown was already gone: all the department stores, for example, including Root's. (Long gone, of course, was the Jakle saloon and, for that matter, the building that once housed a local sales office for Columbus Mining.) Although the Terre Haute House would be missed, much of value would remain. More than a few landmark buildings and even a few building ensembles still stand: street scenes that suggest what the city's downtown had once been.

Of course, there were new things to be seen in downtown, confirming that the future would be different from the past. Just north of the Terre Haute House, one could not miss the city's giant basketball arena (built, some say, in homage to Larry Bird). The city's skyline is now dominated by high-rise dormitories, Indiana State University having expanded well into the business district. The university is now Terre Haute's largest employer. Banking still thrives downtown, both in old and new buildings, but, if you want to find retailing, you have to drive several miles south (down the Third Street commercial strip, today's US 41). There, at the I-70 interchange, you will find a giant shopping mall.

The Midwest continues to change. How could we expect it not to? Nonetheless, the region's landscapes and places may be changing less rapidly, and less dramatically, than in other parts of the nation, especially the South and the West. It is not, in other words, totally impossible for a Midwesterner, or a visitor to the region, to anchor old memories in what remains of familiar places. Perhaps that is why the Midwest remains, for me, my kind of place.

GALLERY
The Midwest in Pictures

PHOTOGRAPHS BY JOHN A. JAKLE

Figure 1.

POSTCARD VIEW WEST ALONG WABASH AVENUE, TERRE HAUTE, INDIANA, CIRCA 1910.

This was the Terre Haute that Theodore Dreiser visited in writing *A Hoosier Holiday* (1916). Black smoke drifts over downtown. The high sulfur content of western Indiana coal filled the city's air with a kind of rotten-egg smell, an odor given added flavor by distilleries and wood treatment plants, as I well remember from childhood summers spent in the city during the 1940s. Shown in the distance is the Root Dry Goods Co. Department Store, behind which looms the tower of the Vigo County courthouse. Below is Wabash Avenue, the old National Road that, beginning in the 1920s, carried the newly marked US 40 through town. Spread out along the eastern bank of the Wabash River on an elevated "savannah"—as early travel writers termed it—Terre Haute was, like many other river cities in the Midwest, mainly a river-crossing place. The city's bridges were what counted. The city turned its back on the river, its downtown developing eastward along the axis of Wabash Avenue. Except for the buildings at the lower left and the distant courthouse, a very different scene greets the eye today: a few new office buildings, a parking garage, and parking lots. Lots of them.

Street Scene Looking West from top of Trust Building, Terre Haute, Indiana

Figure 2.

POSTCARD VIEW OF THE UNITED COAL COMPANY MINE,
EAST OF CHRISTOPHER, ILLINOIS, 1910.

Here is where my mother's people, the Allais family, solidified their position on
the lower rungs of the capitalist class. Traveling in France about this time, my
mother's father, Edward Allais, sent postcards home to her sister, Irma. One
card depicted young girls sorting coal in a mine near Lille, the area from which
the Allais family had emigrated thirty years before. "Well Cherette," he wrote,
"you will see on this card how young girls have to work in France. It broke my
heart when I saw it. It is a disgrace to France." It was also a reminder of how
much life had improved for my mother's people in America.

The mine shown in this photo was fully modern—not just mechanized, but
all-electric. The coal produced here was shipped by rail to Chicago and other
cities across the Midwest. Although the mine closed shortly after World War II,
the brick building in the lower right of the photo still stands.

Figure 3.

426 WILLOW STREET, TERRE HAUTE, INDIANA, 2004.

Following family tradition, I always reference by number the houses where I once lived: 426 (Willow), 286 (McKinley), 1105 (Brighton), 405 (West Michigan), and so forth. It is, perhaps, a quintessentially Midwestern habit. Where else in the world are so many places so well numbered? Section 13, Township 6, Range 4. First, Second, or Third Street. Zip codes only add to the fun. It was not until I traveled in Europe that I realized why this particular house so appealed to my grandfather. First, it was of brick, not frame. In the European tradition, brick spoke not only of affluence, but of stability and permanence. And the brick used here was not just any brick but of a finish and a color fully reminiscent of houses he had known as a boy in France. Originally, 426 also had an elaborate orange tile roof very much in the tradition of the Low Countries. Today, the house sits in a deteriorating neighborhood; the view here is taken from the rear, across what is now a vacant lot. Also on Willow Street lived the Root family, owners of the department store downtown as well as a local glass factory that produced for Coca-Cola the signature "hobbleskirt" Coke bottle. Next door to the Allais family lived a Swedish immigrant, the designer of that bottle. Monday through Friday, the Root limousine stopped to pick him up—the factory owner and honored employee going off to work together. It was only to the Roots, however, that Coke bottle royalties were paid.

Figure 4.

THE GRAVE OF FELIX JAKLE, JEFFERSON STREET CEMETERY,
EFFINGHAM, ILLINOIS, 1989.

His great-grandson's shadow is cast across his grave. The Jakle plot sits very close to US 40. For decades I had driven past it without knowing of its existence. Land records I perused at the local courthouse revealed that Felix, Constantine, and Valentine Jakle once owned the acreage immediately south of where they lay buried—land crossed by the National Road, the Vandalia Railroad (today's CSX), and Salt Creek. It was there that they built and operated a brewery. I first entered that property from the highway through the railroad viaduct that spans the creek. Steep bluffs, heavily wooded, contained my view, directing it along the axis of a narrow floodplain cropped in corn. I stood transfixed. The personal symbolism seemed profound. Here was salt, my dissertation topic when in graduate school. Here was the roadside that dominated much of my subsequent scholarship. Here was the pastoral ideal that had so energized Midwestern history. Here was the small town. Expensive new houses lined the bluffs, developers having been attracted by the view. This microcosm encompassed much of what interested me as a geographer.

Figure 5.

PORTION OF A WALL MURAL (PAINTED IN THE 1960s BY JOHN JOSEPH LASKA) IN THE EUGENE V. DEBS HOUSE, TERRE HAUTE, INDIANA.

Relations between capitalists and organized labor were always tense in Terre Haute, a railroad, iron foundry, and coal mining center. Conflict came to a climax in the 1939 general strike, during which I, opportunely, was born in the city's Union Hospital. My mother's father, the coal operator, was overheard on the telephone giving a friend the news: "They named him John, after John L. Lewis, by God!" Of course, I was named for my father (as he had been named for his) and not for the leader of the United Mines Workers of America. My father, however, did carry the name of a labor leader. Debs was his middle name, after Eugene V. Debs, a family friend. My father was at Terre Haute's Union Depot (and was later a guest at the Debs house) the night Eugene V. Debs came home from the Atlanta Penitentiary. Debs had been incarcerated for vigorously opposing the nation's involvement in World War I. As the socialist presidential candidate, he had received while in prison nearly a million votes, three percent of the total cast. As an elementary school teacher in Detroit, my mother would one day join a union and walk a picket line, much to her initial chagrin. And my wife, Cynthia, librarian at Central High School in Champaign, Illinois, would be her union's building steward for more than a decade.

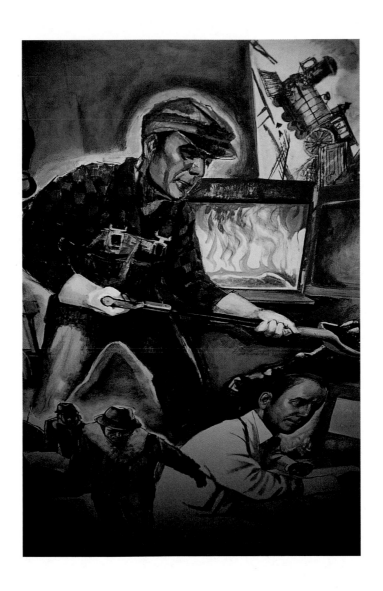

Figure 6.

POSTCARD SCHEMATIC OF THE ANTICIPATED REDEVELOPMENT
ALONG THE ST. LOUIS, MISSOURI, WATERFRONT, CIRCA 1960.

Places change. Indeed, the St. Louis waterfront of today looks very much like
the one projected in this postcard a half century ago. Modernism dictated that
old things, especially things obsolete, needed to be demolished, clearing the
way for progressive new things that spoke forcefully of economic and thus
social betterment. The oldest section of St. Louis, which my father had known
so well as a boy, was largely cleared away in a frenzy of government-sponsored
"urban renewal." The old city was replaced by a riverfront park containing the
giant Gateway Arch by Eero Saarinen, a fixture intended to symbolize the city's
early role as "Gateway to the West." After the Civil War, my great grandfather,
Jacob Bischoff, began making wagons near where Busch Stadium (pictured
here, but now replaced by a new stadium) stood. It was also along the Mississippi River waterfront that my father's uncle, Edward Jakle, worked as a locomo-
tive engineer. Edward, a bachelor and dedicated baseball fan, worked seven
days a week, using his accumulated time off to watch the St. Louis Browns play
their home games. One remembers that, early in the twentieth century, St. Louis
was "first in shoes, first in booze, and last in the American League." Today, city
pride sustains the Cardinals of the National League.

Figure 7.

THE DETROIT RIVER AT DETROIT, MICHIGAN, 1956.

Here is one of my earliest photographs, evidence of my first trip out to photo-graph "landscape." Having taken the tunnel under the Detroit River to Windsor, in Canada, I came back by way of the Ambassador Bridge. This is where one goes in the age of NAFTA (the North American Free Trade Agreement) to see engines, fenders, car bodies, and, indeed, completed autos being transported, factories either side of the border being linked in "just-in-time" truck delivery. Today, the bridge's four traffic lanes are jammed day and night. In 1956, how-ever, the bridge was lightly used, and I was able to stop, linger, and admire the view. In the foreground is the Bob-lo boat on its way to a down-river amusement park. Detroit's waterfront was fully dominated by railroads, factories, and ware-houses, just as in St. Louis. Away from the river, however, Detroit was noted for its pleasant tree-lined streets: a city of mainly single-family homes. "Detroit the Picturesque," the city was once called. Very little is left of that early twentieth-century place. "Detroit the Dynamic" is what the city came to be nicknamed. Industrial Detroit proved ever so changeful and not always for the better.

Figure 8.

NIGHTTIME POSTCARD VIEW, HUDSON MOTOR CAR FACTORY,

DETROIT, MICHIGAN, CIRCA 1948.

In driving between home and downtown Detroit, I went regularly past or through (depending upon the street I chose) Hudson's industrial complex. The postcard's caption reads: "Founded in 1909, Hudson is one of the automobile industry's leaders, having produced over 3,000,000 automobiles. These plants employ over 20,000 people in more than 3,000,000 sq. ft. of manufacturing space. Producing the new Hudson: 'the car you step down into.'"

Designed by industrial architect Albert Kahn, the factory was one of the first constructed in the United States of steel-reinforced poured concrete. So solidly was it built that its demolition in the 1960s (after operations had been moved to Kenosha, Wisconsin) nearly bankrupted Hudson's successor firm, American Motors. The 1967 riot—precipitated by decades of racial discrimination against blacks—greatly accelerated the move of whites and white businesses to the suburbs. Through the 1970s, the city of Detroit lost more than 200,000 jobs. By 1990, city government had become the owner of more than twenty percent of the city's real estate as whole neighborhoods were abandoned. By 2000, the city's population had shrunk to fewer than 900,000, half the 1950 population peak. Today, after decades of standing vacant, this site, although containing a small shopping center in one corner, remains largely undeveloped.

Hudson Motor Car Company. Detroit. Mich.

Figure 9.

NEAR EAST SIDE, DETROIT, MICHIGAN, 1965.

Witness here the demise of Detroit's once vigorous African-American business district, the area derisively dubbed by many whites as "Paradise Valley." Awaiting demolition through federally subsidized urban renewal, a corner retail building shelters a pickup card game. Here was a neighborhood originally German, then Greek and Italian. In addition, surviving here into the 1960s was Detroit's last French-speaking Roman Catholic Church, a holdover from the city's earliest era. But first, during World War I, and then again, during World War II, African-Americans, attracted in large numbers to the city by assembly-line work, settled here. Denied access to housing beyond this area, black families doubled up, and doubled up again, in homes originally constructed for single families. A class of white landlords milked the housing stock while charging blacks high rents. But was Paradise Valley really the slum that planners and politicians claimed, thus to justify neighborhood destruction? There was, in fact, viable community life rooted here, as was much of the Motor City's music and entertainment scene.

Figure 10.

STATE STREET, LOOKING NORTH, CHICAGO, ILLINOIS, 1977.

In comparison with Detroit, Chicago always seemed truly cosmopolitan. Detroit was a place of work where raw materials, labor, and imagination combined to produce cars. Of course, Detroit made other things, but compared to Chicago it was really an overgrown single-industry town: a place where the assembly-line mass production of motor cars set a negative social tone fully evident in how different kinds of people related to one another. In Detroit, managers tended to exploit employees, labor leaders to exploit union members, landlords to exploit tenants, car makers to exploit customers, and so on. Pride was taken in an everyday dog-eat-dog approach.

Chicago seemed, at least to me, more successful at masking such behavior. Chicago was not only industrially diverse, but also a financial center and a wholesaling and retailing place of great importance. Downtown Detroit was small; Chicago's downtown was large. Detroit's skyline was impressive; Chicago's even more so. Indeed, Chicago was said to have invented the skyscraper. As pictured here, shoppers throng Chicago's principal retail thoroughfare, although downtown merchants were already feeling the negative impact of competing suburban shopping centers. Chicago's Loop (the downtown area inside the loop of the elevated transit system) is remarkably viable today. State Street still generates active street life, quite in contrast to Detroit's Woodward Avenue.

Figure 11.

THE RAVENSWOOD LINE OF THE ELEVATED TRANSIT SYSTEM,
CHICAGO, ILLINOIS, 1989.

When I took this photograph, Chicago's North Side was in the early throes of what would prove to be a vigorous revival. New post-industrial jobs, concentrated largely in new downtown high-rise buildings, had begun to generate a market for close-in living. Many people put off by long commutes (and the increased gridlock on city freeways and suburban highways) began to gentrify older, center-city neighborhoods. Increased affluence translated into new demand for goods and services. Accordingly, a whole new retail infrastructure was created not only along the central city's traditional commercial strips, but also where many industrial buildings had stood. Some factories and warehouses were converted to retailing or refit for apartment and condominium living. Today, gentrification is also happening on the city's near West Side and near South Side, areas more substantially impacted by decline induced by racism and its economic, political, and social correlates. Middle- and upper-middle income African-Americans, Latinos, and Asian-Americans, and not just affluent whites, are involved in Chicago's neighborhood resurgence. In the 1960s, only the automobile seemed to harken the city's future. Now, mass transit has again become an important player.

Figure 12.

POSTCARD VIEW NORTH ALONG MICHIGAN AVENUE, CHICAGO, ILLINOIS, CIRCA 1930.

On the right is Grant Park beyond which, out of view, is Lake Michigan. On the left, beyond the mansard roof of the Blackstone Hotel, stands the McCormick Building where the Columbus Mining Company occupied a suite of offices. Down the street is Orchestra Hall, where Arthur Allais, my grandfather's brother and partner in the coal business, eventually conducted his Sunday services as a Methodist minister. For his work with Chicago's French-speaking community, Arthur was honored with membership in the French Legion. Today, much that is pictured here still remains. The building ensemble that lines Michigan Avenue is thought to be an important part of the city's distinctive iconography. Accordingly, the area has been designated a landmark district.

252. MICHIGAN BOULEVARD, LOOKING NORTH, SEEN FROM AEROPLANE, CHICAGO.   THE DRAKE.

THE BLACKSTONE.

Figure 13.

SKYSCRAPER REFLECTION, OAK STREET, CHICAGO, ILLINOIS, 1998.

Carrying a camera became central to my experiencing "landscape" and "place." From the 1960s through the 1990s, so much of what I photographed seemed to carry negative implications. In cities across the Midwest, extensive areas were being destroyed, if not through urban renewal then through the development of freeways. Neighborhoods, racked by white flight, suffered physical blight. Impoverished new residents—those traditionally denied good jobs and quality schooling, among other opportunities—moved in to fall victim to slum landlords, unsympathetic mortgage lenders, and unscrupulous realtors, among others. Declining affluence, declining real estate values, and declining tax revenues undermined every big city's ability to maintain public infrastructure, control crime, and otherwise promote public welfare. The downtowns of many cities became little more than tall buildings surrounded by parking lots, so many activities having been lost to the suburbs. Detroit epitomized that change. Chicago, thanks to mass transit, was able to retain a viable central business district—although, as the photo shows, it was also very much auto-oriented. Only through proverbial rose-colored glasses (or, in the case of the photographer, through deliberate search for the photogenic) could cities in the late-twentieth century Midwest be viewed uncritically.

Figure 14.

AERIAL VIEW OF A NEW SUBDIVISION, ELMHURST, ILLINOIS, 1977.

The automobile's impact on landscapes and places in America was nowhere greater than in new suburban subdivisions where car ownership was absolutely necessary. The curvilinearity of the street grid, its round cul-de-sacs complemented by the round backyard swimming pools, is what caught my eye while sitting at the window of an airliner beginning its descent to Chicago's O'Hare Airport. Although, strictly speaking, none of the houses are alike, a sense of profound uniformity nonetheless plays out. The houses were all built at essentially the same time in the same ranch style. Each is similarly set back from a street across an open lawn, and each has a driveway and a garage. This is what I call a "wallpaper landscape." With wallpaper, once you comprehend the pattern in one corner of a wall, you know how it plays out everywhere. The pattern seen here results from standardized building codes and zoning ordinances. Especially influential in such homogenization were the mandates of Federal Housing Administration and Veterans Administration mortgage guarantee programs. My father, who sold mortgage insurance in his later years, was very much encouraged by the nation's booming suburbs.

Figure 15.

"EDGE-CITY" DEVELOPMENT NEAR O'HARE AIRPORT,
CHICAGO, ILLINOIS, 1991.

The downtown areas of many cities were substantially remade in the last three decades of the twentieth century. So, too, were new business districts created in the suburbs, many of them built from scratch on what previously had been open farmland. Variously called "urban villages" or "edge cities," they contain office, hotel, retail, residential, and entertainment functions. Everything is fully auto-oriented; a new parking deck, for example, is under construction in this scene. Chicago has several such centers, including those at Schaumberg, Naperville, Oak Brook, and Itasca. In the Detroit area are Southfield and Troy. In the St. Louis area is Clayton, and outside Kansas City, Missouri, is Overland Park, Kansas. I find these places glitzy and thus impressive to a point, but they prompt in me little affection. It is corporate America at its unimaginative best.

Figure 16.

NEAR WEST SIDE, CINCINNATI, OHIO, 1993.

Important nineteenth-century landmarks, such as City Hall and the Roman Catholic cathedral on the left and the city's leading synagogue on the right, sit as isolates surrounded by parked cars. Cincinnati (once dubbed "Porkopolis") was the largest meat packing center in the United States until replaced by Chicago in the 1850s. But Cincinnati remained an economically diverse industrial city with important gateway functions. Into the city came tobacco and other farm products from the Upper South as well as coal and other raw materials, especially from Appalachia. Products of the nation's manufacturing belt were distributed southward in return. Cincinnati, located midway between Pittsburgh and the Ohio River's confluence with the Mississippi at Cairo, Illinois, competed with St. Louis to be the mid-continent's principal city. Both places lost to Chicago once railroading displaced steamboats and canals as the most important transportation arteries at mid-continent. Today, however, it is automobility that energizes Cincinnati, as the parked cars testify.

Figure 17.

JOBBER'S CANYON, OMAHA, NEBRASKA, 1989.

While developers in some cities began rehabilitating old buildings, those in
Omaha continued to tear them down. As in Cincinnati, only a small portion of
Omaha's once extensive warehouse and wholesaling district survives. From the
1960s through the 1990s, civic leaders in most of the Midwest's cities came to
anticipate only continued blight and decline in older sections. To be saved, they
argued, these sections needed to be modernized: old structures were to be
torn down and replaced with new. To be saved, in other words, cities had to be
destroyed. Newness, pure and simple, it was argued, would not only symbolize,
but also enable progress. Along the Missouri River in downtown Omaha today,
a vast park-like expanse of greenery stretches uninterrupted save for clusters of
low-rise office buildings amid parking lots. This new landscape speaks not just
of automobility, but of the kind of American pastoralism configured in recent
decades in the nation's auto-oriented suburbs. Downtown Omaha, we might
say, has been "suburbanized."

Figure 18.

HENRY FORD MUSEUM, DEARBORN, MICHIGAN, 2003.

As I took this photo, two granddaughters were wandering around looking at cars very much as I had done some fifty years earlier. When I first saw the museum, it emphasized nineteenth-century farm implements, housing one of the world's largest collections of plows and harrows, for example. It also housed a world-class collection of stationary steam engines. Henry Ford was an avid anti-quarian. History was "bunk," he supposedly said. What he meant was that writ-ten history could not be trusted. Artifacts! That was what he thought spoke honestly of the past. Artifacts spoke for themselves about how people had lived. Today, most of the farm implements and steam engines are gone. Old cars were what visitors came to value most, so the museum now emphasizes the motor car and its impact on American life. As pictured here, antique autos are arranged in a manner suggestive of the traditional auto plant assembly line.

Figure 19.

VIEW FROM 286 MCKINLEY ROAD, GROSSE POINTE FARMS, MICHIGAN, 1971.

This was what I saw when I looked out of my bedroom window. Henry Ford II grew up in a mansion a little more than a mile away, his bedroom contrived in streamline modern style. And he went on to oversee the making of motor cars—many of them, at first, very much streamlined like his room. I grew up in room with a view but one otherwise fully unpretentious as to style. The furniture was cast off from Terre Haute's 426 Willow Street. I spent a lot of time gazing out, a pastime that complemented my looking out of train and car windows. What I saw was a latter-day version of a French eighteenth-century long-lot farm that once fronted on nearby Lake St. Clair. As I understood it, the farm was bought in the late-nineteenth century by a lumber baron whose wealth had derived from the cutting down of forests in northern Michigan. On the lakefront, he built a summer house and then a permanent estate house, selling the back of the property in the early-twentieth century to one of Detroit's wealthy automakers. He, in turn, undertook to subdivide the land for houses appropriate to Detroit's growing management class. Lots averaged forty feet in width and eighty feet in depth, the houses separated by narrow driveways. When I sold my parents' house, I was surprised to find (although I should not have been) various restrictive covenants attached to the property deed. Front yards were to remain open, lawns thus to coalesce park-like. Property owners were forbidden to erect walls and fences or even grow hedges there. But most arresting of all were the Caucasian-only and the Christian-only clauses. Dictated was a residential geography of privileged exclusion.

Figure 20.

GRAIN ELEVATOR, TUTTLE, NORTH DAKOTA, 1994.

Pure functionality tends to govern what one sees in the Midwest, save in elite suburbs, such as Grosse Pointe, or in parks, cemeteries, or other institutional landscapes, such as university campuses. Utility particularly governs much of what one sees in the Midwest's small towns, especially along the railroad tracks or where railroad right-of-ways once ran. Nothing symbolizes the Midwestern small town quite like the region's grain elevators. Spaced at regular intervals along the railroads but approached today largely along paralleling highways, they are usually the tallest, if not the largest, structures around. They announce towns at a distance— "cathedrals of the plains," architect Le Corbusier called them. At the elevators, grain is graded as to moisture and cleanliness and then lifted either by conveyer belt or suction tube to be dropped into storage bins— form closely following function. Here, form clearly reflects changing technology. Recent structural additions reflect the post-World War II shift from the belt to the tube and from buildings fabricated on site to those prefabricated in distant factories.

Figure 21.

MAIN STREET, PLATTSMOUTH, NEBRASKA, 2003.

Like the family farm, the Midwestern small town was a kind of mythic place in the American consciousness. It was in the small community that American democracy was once thought to be anchored fundamentally. As the nation's cities boomed, however, Midwestern small-town life, like the region's farm life, came to be stereotyped negatively. Demeaned as parochial and staid, perhaps it actually was. But I cannot help but wonder why urban Americans, over most of the twentieth century, worked so diligently to replicate around their cities suburbs that appeared so rural and small-town-like. Depicted here is a main street typical of the Midwest. Traditionally, Main Street was a place of commerce juxtaposed between farm field and city market. It was what symbolized the small town as a "central place."

Here at Plattsmouth, cars and trucks are angle-parked at the curb and storefronts are oriented to a nearby courthouse. There are probably too many courthouses in the Midwest today. The drawing of county boundaries and the locating of courthouses originally reflected the realities of horse-drawn transport: the ability of farm families to get to and from their county seats by wagon in a day. Across much of the region today, the automobile has reduced such travel to a matter of minutes.

Figure 22.

I-35 CORRIDOR SOUTH OF DOWNTOWN MINNEAPOLIS, MINNESOTA, 1994.

Transportation influenced not only the location of urban places, but also their internal layout. In Minneapolis, a central business district was built up adjacent to the Falls of St. Anthony on the Mississippi River, which provided power for grain milling, among other activities. This district was reinforced by railroad connectivity in the city's earliest years. Outward from downtown and oriented to streetcars lines, residential neighborhoods were developed, each attracting and holding residents of varying social characteristics—including ethnic/racial, occupational, and income—for varying periods of time. The city's more affluent classes led the way into the suburbs, especially after World War I, with suburban municipalities being added, decade by decade, around the central city. Whether conceptualized in terms of concentric growth rings, sectors of shared land use, or multiple nuclei of varying land uses, many morphological features are shared by all Midwestern cities. It is, perhaps, concentric-ring zonation that today's freeway motorists most readily notice. Downtown skylines loom up ahead with neighborhoods, glimpsed along freeway margins, becoming progressively older as downtown is approached.

Figure 23.

TOW ON THE OHIO RIVER, OPPOSITE VEVAY, INDIANA, 2000.

Initially, the Ohio River was the great central corridor of development in the Midwest. With Kentucky, Tennessee, and what is today West Virginia opened to westward settlement, frontier development then swept into southern Ohio, southern Indiana, southern Illinois, and, eventually, eastern Missouri before sweeping across the Great Lakes. After the Civil War, economic energy definitely shifted north to the lakes, and it was on their shores that most of the mid-continent's heavy industry developed, since iron ore and coal (among other raw materials) were cheaply conveyed there. The Ohio River lost its primacy in transportation and came to be thought of more as a dividing line between North and South. Slowly, the idea of a Middle West (or Midwest) supplanted earlier sectional designators, including the "Old Northwest," once seen as centering on Chicago. Today, the movement of giant tows, transporting coal, grain, petroleum, and other bulk commodities, brings a sense of spectacle to the inland rivers. As pictured, two fishermen pause to watch.

Figure 24.

FORTY-THIRD STREET, KANSAS CITY, KANSAS, 1995.

Properties are developed oriented to lines of movement but only to the extent that those properties are accessible to traffic flow. Midwestern landscapes have been variously organized for people and goods moving along waterways, along railroads, and now along auto roads, including both city streets and rural highways. The motor car and motor truck count most today. Pictured here is a big-city commercial strip. It might be anywhere in the Midwest or anywhere in the nation for that matter. It just happens to be in Kansas. While the roadway dominates the motorist's view, the roadside clamors for attention, first and foremost through exaggerated curbside signs that mark entry to driveways and parking lots. Roadside architecture tends to be highly standardized, both in appearance and functionality, especially where corporate franchise chains prevail. Here, the signature architecture of the fast-food industry is most prominent. Signage, logos, color schemes, architectural design, and even landscaping are coordinated for ready customer recognition, location to location, across networks of look-alike stores. This is the stuff of what has come to be called "place-product-packaging."

Figure 25.

INTERIOR OF THE MERCHANT'S NATIONAL BANK, GRINNELL, IOWA, 1984.

Whereas corporatization has brought much homogeneity to Midwestern landscapes and places, much that is distinctive can also be seen. Louis Sullivan, a
pioneer architect in the creation of Chicago's tall buildings, settled late in his
career for modest commissions, such as this 1914 bank building. His designs
first anticipated and then followed the thinking of Frank Lloyd Wright, whose
Prairie Style buildings brought to the Midwest a distinctive architecture region-
ally based. The relatively few examples of Prairie Style architecture extant today
serve to remind Midwesterners of what might have been early in the twentieth
century. Culturally as well as economically, however, the Midwest was dependent on (even colonial to) the Northeast. Boston, New York, Philadelphia, and
other cities took their aesthetic cues very much from Europe, so popular tastes
in the Midwest turned more to traditional European design motifs as well. Call it
an inferiority complex, if you like.

Figure 26.

MEMORIAL STADIUM, UNIVERSITY OF ILLINOIS, CHAMPAIGN, ILLINOIS, 2004.

Taking in the American scene is very much a spectator sport. We aspire to be active players in one or another game of life, but, for much of what goes on around us, it is more a matter of making sure we fit in as observers. I admire people capable of taking even the most mundane of events, and the most common of places, and internalizing them as a kind of spectacle around which fuller comprehension and appreciation can accrue. Taught on the nation's playing fields is respect for the details of intentionality and execution: lessons useful, no doubt, in orchestrating the game of life. Perhaps therein lies some of the rationalization for the Midwest's extravagant investments in sport stadia, whether they court basketball (long considered a regional sport specialty), football, baseball, or even ice hockey. Loyalty to the region is, for many Midwesterners, filtered through team loyalty: the Badgers of Wisconsin, Buckeyes of Ohio State, Bulldogs of Minnesota-Duluth, Cornhuskers of Nebraska, Coyotes of South Dakota, Cyclones of Iowa State, Fighting Sioux of North Dakota, Gophers of Minnesota, Hawkeyes of Iowa, Hoosiers of Indiana, Fighting Illini of Illinois, Jayhawks of Kansas, Spartans of Michigan State, Tigers of Missouri, Wildcats of Kansas State and Northwestern, and Wolverines of Michigan, among the many others.

Figure 27.

HAMILTON PRODUCE CO., A FARM SERVICE STORE, BLOOMFIELD, IOWA, 1990.

What kind of place is this? And how might it be important? Most Midwestern towns were, and still are, farm towns, very much dependent on a rural economy. It was to the railroad siding in town where farmers brought their crops at harvest time. It was in town where they bought their seed and filled other needs. Town was where farm families shopped, and, when things were ordered by catalog, it was to the town's post office where they picked up packages (and local news and gossip), at least before the advent of free rural mail delivery. As automobile ownership became widespread, farm families increasingly oriented to small towns for church and school. In central Illinois, farmers are grain producers, selling their mostly corn and soybean harvests through local grain elevators. In southeastern Iowa, however, farmers feed much of their grain (especially the corn) to hogs or other livestock and then sell the animals to stockyards and packing plants. Traditional "Corn Belt" agriculture (fattening animals in feed lots) shifted ever westward during the twentieth century and, today, centers in the Great Plains. The nation's food supply is now dominated by a relatively few big corporations. They control the supply of feed, seed, fertilizer, and other agricultural raw materials. They control the manufacturing and marketing of finished foodstuffs. Size through vertical integration has come to the fore. But pictured here is a traditional farm service store, small in size and still operating at the "Main Street" scale.

Figure 28.

FARM FIELD NEAR WILLIAMSVILLE, ILLINOIS, 1992.

The rural Midwest is deceptively fertile. As a city person, I am repeatedly amazed at the fecundity, even though I know how artificial it has actually become, especially through the massive application of fertilizer. And, in my area, the land is fully drained, most farm fields being underlain by tile. One is not really seeing nature in this scene. Landscapes in east-central Illinois, as across much of the Midwest, seem fully rationalized, especially in the shape and organization of farm fields where the section-line grid plays out so predictably. Everything seems to meet at right angles: roads, fences (where there are fences), and even soybeans and corn planted row upon row. The geometry of the landscape suggests a map as large as the landscape itself. Farmhouses stand along roads oriented to the cardinal directions. Inside, rooms are similarly oriented, as is much of the furniture. In the farmer's bedroom, likely the only thing canted at the diagonal is the alarm clock.

Figure 29.

SPRING PLANTING NEAR CLARENCE, ILLINOIS, 2000.

The rural Midwest still reflects the ideals of Jeffersonian democracy. American citizenship, especially when sustained by farm ownership, was seen ideally as rooted in the working of the soil. Of course, today's agriculture, guided from corporate offices in such cities as Omaha, Minneapolis, and Chicago, is big, to say the least. The average farm in Illinois grew from 242 acres in 1969 to 470 acres in 2002. But cash-grain farms with more than $100,000 in sales (the approximate threshold for sustained profitability) now average some 1,600 acres in size. The number of farms in Illinois declined from approximately 124,000 in 1969 to fewer than 73,000 in 1999. Like mining, farming became a fully extractive enterprise. Taking biomass from the soil and consuming ground water, it extracts in other ways, as well, more than it puts back. It is a business largely dependent upon petroleum, not just to fuel tractors and other equipment, but to provide the chemical base for fertilizers and insecticides (that encourage plant growth) and herbicides (that ensure efficient machine operation). What we eat is not only engineered for size, appearance, and taste, but also to fit the demands of modern harvesting. Soybeans are being planted here, thirty-six rows at a time. More than 2,000 acres will be planted in a few day's time.

Figure 30.

OLD ORDER AMISH FARM, NEAR FARMERSVILLE, OHIO, 1991.

Among the Old Order Amish in Ohio's Holmes County, one can see pastoral landscapes highly reminiscent of farming everywhere in the Midwest three generations ago. Horse power enables the Amish to remain symbolically, if not actually, self-sufficient as a community, their dependence on an outside world (the world now dominated by giant agribusinesses, for example) seemingly minimized. Near Farmersville, small family farms are alive and well, although considerably sustained by outside work. Farm families also earn supplementary income from various artisan crafts. Because Amish landscapes appear caught in something of a time warp, tourists are attracted. It is they who buy the quilts, the oak furniture, and other products that Amish households produce. Amish communities are scattered throughout the Midwest, although the largest are in eastern Ohio and northern Indiana.

Figure 31.

US 40, THE OLD NATIONAL ROAD, AT TEUTOPOLIS, ILLINOIS, 1988.

As its name suggests, Teutopolis was and is solidly German-American, being initially settled in the 1850s by Roman Catholics from Oldenburg. The spire of St. Joseph's Church appears in the distance. That church, the convent and seminary that stood adjacent to it, the imposing brick wall that surrounded them all, and the pollarded trees that lined the town's streets suggested to me, as a young traveler, that here was a place "just like Europe." The town's Germanic aspect is quite noticeable today in the orderliness and high levels of maintenance afforded both public and private spaces. This part of Illinois remained predominantly German-speaking through World War I, although each immigrant group, including Lutherans from Saxony and Roman Catholics from Bavaria, spoke very different dialects. Isolated immigrant families, such as the Jakles from Baden, found it expedient to learn English and to do so quickly so as to acculturate to an American mainstream. Martin Jakle, one of my father's uncles, was sufficiently Americanized to be elected sheriff of Effingham County in 1900. Today, the "Wooden Shoes" of Teutopolis excel in high school basketball and other sports, as signs posted at the edge of town proudly attest.

Figure 32.

LAKE MICHIGAN NEAR SOUTH HAVEN, MICHIGAN, 2000.

Few Americans think of the Midwest as having a coastline. Yet the shoreline along the Great Lakes is nearly equivalent in length to either the nation's Atlantic or Pacific coasts, and it is much longer than that of the Gulf of Mexico. In the 1920s, my mother's family, escaping the heat, humidity, and hay fever of the Corn Belt, came regularly to South Haven each August. It was a tradition my family recently revived. Not only do the Great Lakes sustain an important resort industry, but they are vital to the movement of industrial raw materials, such as iron ore (now taconite), coal, limestone, and petroleum. Water drawn from the lakes is vital to oil refining and chemical manufacture as well as to the generation of electric power. Much American and Canadian grain, especially wheat, moves by lake freighter eastward to Buffalo and other ports. Cleveland, Toledo, Detroit, Duluth, Milwaukee, and Chicago became important "seaports" with completion of the St. Lawrence Seaway in 1959. But the resort aspect and picturesque qualities of land meeting water attract the tourists today.

Figure 33.

DAIRY FARM, NEAR ODANAH, WISCONSIN, 1982.

Dairying, hand in hand with hay production, was the predominant farm activity across the northern or Upper Midwest. Along the Midwest's western and northern peripheries, cold and dry climate, respectively, discouraged (or, perhaps, better said, should have discouraged) farming. In the west, much crop land has reverted to pasture, but in the north much pasture land has reverted to forest. The farm pictured here appears to be teetering on the brink of extinction. Lumbering, of course, preceded farming in the northern Great Lakes area, stripping the land of its white pine and other trees. Thus were Midwestern farmsteads, towns, and cities built largely of wood—with Chicago functioning as the principal market for timber. From there, milled lumber was distributed across the nation, especially westward, by rail. So also did Chicago become the Midwest's principal market for fluid milk when, after the Civil War, dairy farms came to dominate northern Illinois and much of Wisconsin. Dairy farmers at some remove from Chicago (or from other important markets, such as Milwaukee and Minneapolis–St. Paul) relied on local cheese factories to create a product that would more profitably withstand long-distance transport.

Figure 34.

LAKE SUPERIOR SHORE, NEAR GRAND MARAIS, MINNESOTA, 2001.

The hard igneous rock of the Canadian Shield extends southward into the United States, interrupted by the glacial trough that is Lake Superior. This area was rich in timber and mineral wealth, especially iron and copper, but never was it an area fully conducive to farming, soils being too meager and growing seasons too short. Today, it is tourism that thrives. Increased affluence, increased leisure time, and increased mobility (especially the increased convenience of highway travel) have wrought a revolution in the "wastelands" of the northern Midwest. Derelict land abandoned from mining, forestry, and farming is now being repackaged as resort property. It was to this far western shore of Lake Superior that French fur traders came to extract wealth in the late seventeenth century. For the first time, resources from North America's mid-continent entered the evolving world economy.

Figure 35.

MAIN STREET, CARTER, SOUTH DAKOTA, 1994.

Interested in how places develop, so also am I interested in how they sometimes wither away: birth and growth, and decline and death, are two sides of
the scholar's landscape coin. As a child, I was intrigued by the romance of the
Western ghost towns, places that had once thrived only to largely disappear. At
the time, the notion applied mainly to mining towns where either gold, silver, or
other minerals had simply played out or where changes in market price had
made mining unprofitable. Today, it is across the Great Plains that new ghost
towns are rapidly appearing. One such place is Carter in South Dakota. Only
one commercial building, long empty, remained standing there the day I
chanced by to take photographs. Over the crest of the hill, out of sight, a few
houses also stood, all but one vacant. Who will remember that here was once a
bustling community of several hundred people? Who will care?

ALDO LEOPOLD'S SHACK NEAR BARABOO, WISCONSIN. PHOTOGRAPH BY
EMILY HUNT AND USED BY PERMISSION.

EPHIGRAPH

Theodore Drieser, *A Hoosier Holiday* (New York: John Lane, 1916), 338.

PREFACE

1. R. Douglas Hurt, "Midwestern Distinctiveness," in Andrew R. L. Cayton and Susan F. Gray, editors, *The American Midwest: Essays on Regional History* (Bloomington: Indiana University Press, 2001), 160–99.

2. Scott Russell Sanders, *Writing From the Center* (Bloomington: Indiana University Press, 1995), 24.

3. John E. Miller, "Lawrence Welk and John Wooden: Midwestern Small-Town Boys Who Never Left Home," *Journal of American Studies* 38 (2004): 110; see, also, John E. Miller, "From the Great Plains to L.A.: The Intersecting Paths of Lawrence Welk and Johnny Carson," *Virginia Quarterly Review* 79 (Spring 2003): 265–80.

4. Miller, "Welk and Wooden," *Journal of American Studies* 38 (2004): 111.

5. Andrew R. L. Cayton and Susan F. Gray, "The Story of the Midwest: An Introduction," in Cayton and Gray, editors, The *American Midwest*, 4.

A HOOSIER HOLIDAY

1. Theodore Dreiser, *A Hoosier Holiday* (New York: John Lane, 1916).

2. My publications with a decidedly Midwestern slant include: John A. Jakle, *Images of the Ohio Valley: A Historical Geography of Travel, 1740 to 1860* (New York: Oxford University Press, 1977); *The American Small Town: Twentieth-Century Place Images* (Hamden, CT: Archon Books, 1982); "Images of Place: Symbolism and the Middle Western Metropolis," in Carl Patton and Barry Checkoway, editors, *The Metropolitan Midwest* (Urbana: University of Illinois Press, 1985), 74–103; "Childhood on the Middle Border: Remembered Small Town America," *Journal of Geography* 85 (July/Aug. 1986): 159–61; "The Ohio Valley Revisited: Images from Nicholas Cresswell and Reuben Gold Thwaites," in Robert L. Reid, editor, *Always a River: The Ohio River in the American Experience* (Bloomington: Indiana University Press, 1991), 32–66; "Social Stereotypes and Place Images: People on the Trans-Appalachian Frontier as Viewed by Travelers," in Leo Zonn, editor, *Place Images in the Media* (Savage, MD: Rowman and Littlefield, 1991), 83–103; "Toward a Geographical History of Indiana: Landscape and Place in the Historical Imagination," *Indiana Magazine of History*, 89 (Sept. 1993): 177–209; "Travelers' Impressions of the National Road," in Karl Raitz, editor, *The National Road* (Baltimore: The Johns Hopkins University Press, in association with the Center for American Places, 1996), 227–308; and "Towns to Visit: Sights (Sites) to See," in Curtis M. Roseman and Elizabeth Roseman, editors, *Grand Excursions on the Upper Mississippi River: Places, Landscapes, and Identity* (Iowa City: University of Iowa Press, 2004), 87–101.

3. Dreiser, *A Hoosier Holiday*, 25.

4. Ibid, 69.

5. These publications include: John A. Jakle, *The Tourist: Travel in Twentieth-Century North America* (Lincoln: University of Nebraska

Press, 1985); "Landscapes Redesigned for the Automobile," in Michael Conzen, editor, *The Making of the American Landscape* (Boston: Unwin Hyman, 1990), 293–310; with Keith A. Sculle, *The Gas Station in America* (Baltimore: The Johns Hopkins University Press, in association with the Center for American Places, 1994); with Keith A. Sculle and Jefferson S. Rogers, *The Motel in America* (Baltimore: The Johns Hopkins University Press, in association with the Center for American Places, 1996); with Keith A. Sculle, *Fast Food: Roadside Restaurants in the Automobile Age* (Baltimore: The Johns Hopkins University Press, in association with the Center for American Places, 1999); "Pioneer Roads: America's Early Twentieth-Century Named Highways," *Material Culture* 32 (Summer 2000): 1–22; with Keith A. Sculle, *Signs in America's Auto Age: Signatures of Landscape and Place* (Iowa City: University of Iowa Press, 2004); with Keith A. Sculle, *Lots of Parking: Land Use in a Car Culture* (Charlottesville: University of Virginia Press, in association with the Center for American Places, 2004); and, with Keith A. Sculle, *Motoring: The Highway Experience in America* (Athens: University of Georgia Press, in association with the Center for American Places at Columbia College Chicago, 2008).

6. Dreiser, *A Hoosier Holiday*, 152.

7. See Sherwood Anderson, *Winesburg, Ohio* (New York: Random House, 1910), and Sinclair Lewis, *Main Street* (New York: Harcourt, 1920).

8. Dreiser, *A Hoosier Holiday*, 77.

9. See John A. Jakle, "America's Small Town/Big City Dialectic," *Journal of Cultural Geography* 18 (Spring/Summer 1999): 1–27.

10. Dreiser, *A Hoosier Holiday*, 247.

11. Ibid., 402.

12. Ibid., 451.

13. Ibid., 257.

14. Ibid., 266.

15. Ibid., 335.

16. Theodore Dreiser, *Sister Carrie* (New York: Doubleday, Page, 1900) and *An American Tragedy* (New York: Boni and Liveright, 1925).

17. H. G. Wells, *The Time Machine: An Invention* (New York: Holt, 1895).

SOME FAMILY HISTORY OF MY OWN

1. John Edward Hicks, *Adventures of a Tramp Printer, 1880–1890* (Kansas City, MO: Mid-American Press, 1950), 107–08.

TRAVEL AS A LEARNING EXPERIENCE

1. Years ago, I ventured into the Columbus Museum of Art to see a retrospective exhibit honoring George Bellows, the American genre painter. Bellows grew up in that city and attended Ohio State University. Displayed was a picture of the university's 1909 baseball team, and sitting in the front row next to Bellows was Ed Allais.

2. Geographer John C. Hudson thoroughly explains these changes in *Chicago: A Geography of the City and Its Region* (Santa Fe: The Center for American Places and Chicago: University of Chicago Press, 2006).

3. See Bob Thall, *The New American Village* (Baltimore: The Johns Hopkins University Press, in association with the Center for American Places, 1999).

4. James R. Shortridge, *The Middle West: Its Meaning in American Culture* (Lawrence: University Press of Kansas, 1989).

5. William R. Cronon, *Nature's Metropolis: Chicago and the Great West* (New York: W. W. Norton, 1991); see, also, Michael Conzen,

"The Maturing Urban System in the United States, 1870–1910," *Annals of the Association of American Geographers* 67 (March 1977): 88–108.

TRAVEL AND BEYOND

1. Dean MacCannell, *The Tourist: A New Theory of the Leisure Class* (New York: Schocken, 1976), 92.

2. John Urry, *The Tourist Gaze: Leisure and Travel in Contemporary Societies* (London: Sage, 1990).

3. See John A. Jakle, "American Roadside," in *The Great American Roadside: A New Experience at the Henry Ford Museum* (Dearborn, MI: Henry Ford Museum and Greenfield Village, [2000]), 23–25.

4. For further discussion of the Grosse Pointe "point system," see Kathy Cosseboom, *Grosse Pointe, Michigan: Race Against Race* (East Lansing: Michigan State University Press, 1972), 5–25. For an in-depth discussion of elite suburban landscapes as places of exclusivity, see Stephen R. Higley, *Privilege, Power, and Place: The Geography of the American Upper Class* (Savage, MD: Rowman and Littlefield, 1995), and James S. Duncan and Nancy G. Duncan, *Landscapes of Privilege: The Politics of the Aesthetic in an American Suburb* (New York: Routledge, in association with the Center for American Places, 2004).

5. There is debate as to exactly what Charles W. Wilson, the president of General Motors, said. What he later claimed to have said was: "What was good for the United States was good for General Motors, and vice versa."

A GEOGRAPHER IN THE MIDWEST

1. John C. Hudson, *Plains Country Towns* (Minneapolis: University of Minnesota Press, 1985).

2. See Robert J. Mowitz and Deil S. Wright, "Harper Woods Versus the Ford Expressway: Crashing Suburban Gates," in Mowitz and Wright, editors, *Profiles of a Metropolis* (Detroit: Wayne State University Press, 1962), 465–516.

3. The dissertation stands abridged in John A. Jakle, "Salt on the Ohio Valley Frontier, 1770–1820," *Annals of the Association of American Geographers* 59 (Dec. 1969): 687–709.

4. [James Agee], "The Great American Roadside," *Fortune* 10 (Sept. 1934): 53.

5. The popularity of "spatial analysis," with its focus on spatial distribution or location, did prompt some interest in commercial strip development. For example, see Brian J. L. Berry, "Ribbon Development in the Urban Business Pattern," *Annals of the Association of American Geographers* 49 (June 1959): 149–55. Cultural geographers, for their part, focused early on the visual aesthetics of the roadside. For example, see Peirce F. Lewis, David Lowenthal, and Yi-Fu Tuan, *Visual Blight in America* (Washington, DC: Association of American Geographers, Commission of College Geography, Resource Paper No. 23, 1973). Interest in spatial diffusion (the way things spread geographically through innovation adoption) generated some interest in franchised and other restaurant chains. For example, see Judith W. Meyer and Lawrence A. Brown, "Diffusion Agency Establishment: The Case of Friendly Ice Cream and Public-Sector Diffusion Processes," *SEPS* [Socio-Economic Political Science] 13 (1979): 241–49.

6. For elaboration, see John A. Jakle, "Engaging the American Roadside: Lessons Learned Along the Way," *Bulletin of the Illinois Geographical Society* 42 (Spring 2000): 3–20.

7. See John A. Jakle, "The Camera and Geographical Inquiry," in Stanley D. Brunn, Susan L. Cutter, and J. W. Harrington, editors, *Geography and Technology* (Dordrecht, The Netherlands: Kluwer, 2004), 221–42.

8. For example, see Robert Adams, *Why People Photograph: Selected Essays and Reviews* (New York: Aperture, 1994); Joan M. Schwartz and James R. Ryan, editors, *Picturing Place: Photography and the Geographical Imagination* (London: I. B. Tauris, 2003); Stephen Shore, *The Nature of Photographs* (Baltimore: The Johns Hopkins University Press, in association with the Center for American Places, 1998); and John Szarkowski, *The Photographer's Eye* (New York: The Museum of Modern Art, 1966).

9. Current treatises supportive of the place concept's centrality in geographical thought include Robert David Sack, *Human Territoriality: Its Theory and History* (Cambridge, UK: Cambridge University Press, 1986); R. J. Johnston, *A Question of Place: Exploring the Practice of Human Geography* (Oxford, UK: Blackwell, 1991); and Edward W. Soja, *Thirdspace: Journeys to Los Angeles and Other Real and Imagined Places* (Oxford, UK: Blackwell, 1996).

10. John B. Jackson, "In Search of the Proto-Landscape," in George F. Thompson, editor, *Landscape in America* (Austin: University of Texas Press, 1995), 43.

11. For an introduction to J. B. (John Brinckerhoff) Jackson, see Helen Lefkowitz Horowitz, editor, *Landscape in Sight: Looking at America* (New Haven: Yale University Press, 1997), and Ervin H. Zube, editor, *Landscapes: Selected Writings of J. B. Jackson* (Amherst: University of Massachusetts Press, 1970).

12. For example, see James J. Parsons, "'Now this Matter of Cultural Geography': Notes from Carl Sauer's Last Seminar at Berkeley," in Martin S. Kenzer editor, *Carl O. Sauer: A Tribute* (Corvallis: Oregon State University Press, 1987), 153–63.

13. For example, see J. Nicholas Entrikin, *The Betweenness of Place: Toward a Geography of Modernity* (Baltimore: The Johns Hopkins University Press, in association with the Center for American Places,

1991). For a more popular treatment of the subject, see Winifred Gallagher, *The Power of Place: How Our Surroundings Shape Our Thoughts, Emotions, and Actions* (New York: Harper Perennial, 1993).

14. For example, see James Duncan and David Ley, editors, *Place/Culture/Representation* (London: Routledge, 1993).

15. Jim Harrison, *Off to the Side: A Memoir* (New York: Grove Press, 2002), 129.

16. Andrew R. L. Cayton, "The Anti-Region: Place and Identity in the History of the American Midwest," in Andrew R. L. Cayton and Susan F. Gray, editors, *The American Midwest: Essays on Regional History*, (Bloomington: Indiana University Press, 2001), 148.

THE MIDWEST AS A REGION

1. See John A. Jakle and David Wilson, *Derelict Landscapes: The Wasting of America's Built Environment* (Savage, MD: Rowman and Littlefield, 1992).

2. For further discussion of the rural Midwest, see Sonya Salamon, *Prairie Patrimony: Family Farming and Community in the Midwest* (Chapel Hill: University of North Carolina Press, 1992), and Osha Gray Davidson, *Broken Heartland: The Rise of America's Rural Ghetto* (New York: The Free Press, 1990).

3. Theodore Dreiser, *The Color of a Great City* (New York: John Lane, 1916), 168.

4. John A. Jakle, *The Visual Elements of Landscape* (Amherst: University of Massachusetts Press, 1987).

5. Hasia R. Diner, *Lower East Side Memories: A Jewish Place in America* (Princeton: Princeton University Press, 2000), 129.

RETHINKING THE MIDWEST

1. Sheldon Stomquist, "Prairie Politics and the Landscape of Reform," in Robert F. Sayre, editor, *Recovering the Prairie* (Madison: University of Wisconsin Press, 1999), 110.

2. Andrew R. L. Cayton, "The Anti-Region: Place and Identity in the History of the American Midwest," in Andrew R. L. Clayton and Susan F. Gray, editors, *The American Midwest: Essays on Regional History* (Bloomington: Indiana University Press, 2001), 150.

3. Kathleen Neils Conzen, "Pi-ing the Type: Jane Grey Swisshelm and the Contest of Midwestern Regionality," in Cayton and Gray, editors, *The American Midwest*, 91.

4. Jon Gjerde, "Middleness and the Middle West," in Cayton and Gray, editors, *The American Midwest*, 181.

5. For a discussion of autobiography in geographical scholarship, see Pamela Moss, editor, *Placing Autobiography in Geography* (Syracuse: Syracuse University Press, 2001).

SUGGESTED READINGS

Allen, Barbara, and Thomas J. Schlereth, editors, *Sense of Place: American Regional Cultures* (Lexington: University of Kentucky Press, 1990).

Borowiec, Andrew, *Along the Ohio* (Baltimore: The Johns Hopkins University Press, in association with the Center for American Places, 2000).

_____, *Cleveland: The Flats, the Mill, and the Hills* (Chicago: The Center for American Places at Columbia College Chicago, 2008).

Clayton, Andrew R. L., and Susan F. Gray, editors, *The American Midwest: Essays on Regional History* (Bloomington: Indiana University Press, 2001).

Cronon, William R., *Nature's Metropolis: Chicago and the Great West* (New York: W. W. Norton, 1991).

Davidson, Osha Gray, *Broken Heartland: The Rise of America's Rural Ghetto* (New York: The Free Press, 1990).

Davies, Richard O., Joseph A. Amato, and David R. Pickaske, editors, *A Place Called Home: Writing on the Midwestern Small Town* (Minneapolis: University of Minnesota Press, 2003).

d'Eramo, Marco, translated by Grame Thomson, *The Pig and the Skyscraper: Chicago: A History of Our Future* (London: Verso, 2002).

Dreiser, Theodore, *A Hoosier Holiday* (New York: John Lane, 1916).

Dumas, Gerald, *An Afternoon in Waterloo Park: A Narrative Poem* (Boston: Houghton Mifflin, 1972).

Gallagher, Winifred, *The Power of the Place: How Our Surroundings Shape Our Thoughts, Emotions, and Actions* (New York: Harper Perennial, 1993).

Harrison, Jim, *Off to the Side: A Memoir* (New York: Grove Press, 2002).

Hart, John Fraser, *The Land That Feeds Us* (Charlottesville: University of Virginia Press, 2003).

Hudson, John C., *Across This Land: A Regional Geography of the United States and Canada* (Baltimore: The Johns Hopkins University Press, in association with the Center for American Places, 2002).

_____, *Chicago: A Geography of the City and Its Region* (Santa Fe: The Center for American Places and Chicago: University of Chicago Press, 2006).

_____, *Making the Corn Belt: A Geographical History of Middle Western* Agriculture (Bloomington: Indiana University Press, 1994).

Lippard, Lucy R., *The Lure of the Local: Senses of Place in a Multicentered Society* (New York: The New Press, 1997).

Martone, Michael, *A Place of Sense: Essays in Search of the Midwest* (Iowa City: University of Iowa Press, 1988).

Norris, Kathleen, *Dakota: A Spiritual Geography* (New York: Ticknor and Fields, 1993).

Pichaske, David R., *Seven Midwest Writers of Place* (Iowa City: University of Iowa Press, 2006).

Riley, Robert, "Square to the Road, Hogs to the East," *Places* 2 (1985): 72–79.

Sanders, Scott Russell, *Secrets of the Universe: Scenes from the Journey Home* (Boston: Beacon Press, 1991).

Sayre, Robert F., editor, *Recovering the Prairie* (Madison: University of Wisconsin Press, 1999).

Shortridge, James R., *The Middle West: Its Meaning in American Culture* (Lawrence: University Press of Kansas, 1989).

Thall, Bob, *The New American Village* (Baltimore: The Johns Hopkins University Press, in association with the Center for American Places, 1999).

Thompson, Heather Ann, *Whose Detroit? Politics, Labor, and Race in a Modern American City* (Ithaca: Cornell University Press, 2002).

Zelinsky, Wilbur, "North America's Vernacular Regions," *Annals of the Association of American Geographers* 70 (March 1980): 1–16.

Ziegler, Susy S., with John Fraser Hart, *Landscapes of Minnesota—A Geography* (St. Paul: Minnesota Historical Society Press, 2008).

ACKNOWLEDGMENTS

This book has been a joy to write, it being a kind of summing up of my life as lived in the American Midwest. It has been instructive to think about how I became a dedicated Midwesterner, and how it was that the Midwest might have influenced my career as a geographer. I am most thankful to George F. Thompson, founder and director of the Center for American Places, for suggesting that I undertake this project. Thanks, also, go to family members, and to friends and acquaintances, whose lives in various ways intersected with my own to make storytelling about being a Midwesterner reasonably interesting. I acknowledge with gratitude my academic colleagues, especially at Western Michigan University, Southern Illinois University, Indiana University, and the University of Illinois at Urbana-Champaign, who encouraged (or at least abided) my particular (if not sometimes peculiar) teaching and research interests, many of which focused on the Midwest. Important, also, have been coauthors who, over the years, have helped me explore different facets of the American, if not the Midwestern, experience. I am especially grateful for the love and support of Cynthia Powell Jakle, who over the decades has remained a fellow traveler down many a highway across the Midwest and beyond.

ABOUT THE AUTHOR

John Allais Jakle is a Midwesterner both by birth and residential history. Born in Indiana, raised in Michigan, and college-educated in Michigan, Illinois, and Indiana, he taught for more than three decades in the Department of Geography and the Department of Landscape Architecture at the University of Illinois at Urbana-Champaign. He and his wife, Cynthia, continue to live in Urbana. Jakle is the author or co-author of a dozen books, many of which have Midwestern emphases. Their topics include: the car's impact on travel and tourism in the United States and Canada, the rise of "roadside" America, artificial illumination and the look of American cities after dark, signs as an aspect of landscape and place in America, parking as it impacts landscape in American cities, and the highway experience in America. As well, his publications have focused on: changing small-town America, dereliction in America's built environments, landscape visualization, and landscape representation, especially through photography and postcards. Jakle has long been an avid photographer of the American scene.

ABOUT THE BOOK

My Kind of Midwest was brought to publication in an edition of 2,000 harcover copies, with the generous financial assistance of the Elizabeth Firestone Graham Foundation, Ray Graham, President, and the Friends of the Center for American Places, for which the publisher is most grateful. The text was set in Akzidenz Grotesk, and the paper is Chinese Goldeast, 128 gsm weight. The book was printed and bound in China. For more information about the Center for American Places at Columbia College Chicago, please see page 156.

**FOR THE CENTER FOR AMERICAN PLACES
AT COLUMBIA COLLEGE CHICAGO:**

George F. Thompson, Founder and Director

Susan Arritt, Series Consulting Editor and Manuscript Editor

Brandy Savarese, Associate Editorial Director

Jason Stauter, Operations and Marketing Manager

Christine Hoepfner, Editorial Assistant

Marcie McKinley, Design Assistant

David Skolkin, Book Designer and Art Director

Dave Keck, of Global Ink, Inc., Production Coordinator